Pot-B

CW00505663

Clive Bell

Alpha Editions

This edition published in 2024

ISBN 9789361477782

Design and Setting By

Alpha Editions

www.alphaedis.com

Email - info@alphaedis.com

Contents

FOREWORD

DEAR GEOFFREY WHITWORTH,—Considering for how many ages how many clever people have been complaining of their publishers, you might have supposed that no device for getting one of them into a scrape could have been left untried. Yet, so far as I can remember, no author has had the bright idea of denouncing his publisher, particularly, and by name, as accessory before the fact. I am willing to suspect my memory rather than my profession of being at fault in this matter; but that the practice is uncommon is most certain and that, surely, is very strange. No author thinks twice of saddling his friend, his wife, his mother, or even his mistress with the responsibility of having been the onlie begetter of some feckless cub or monstrous abortion; but on his publisher, the very man he should wish to injure, who ever thought of fastening the offence? Yet you cannot deny, my dear Whitworth, that this book is your fault. I was all for abandoning the project after I had read Mr. Arnold Bennett's volume and recognized how much more readable his journalism was than mine: your reader, I suspect, was of like mind: it was you, and you alone, who, by enlisting my vanity, conquered my pride.

Of course in the end my vanity might have triumphed without you: it is not often or easily beaten.

"Obliged by hunger and request of friends,"

I can imagine myself printing under that classic excuse, which has the merit of being in the grand literary tradition and as disingenuous as another; for in these days an author is not more hungry than every one else, and my friends would have been the first to pardon my silence. You may take it for certain, by the way, that when a man says he is publishing at the instance of two or three friends he means that he is offering the public what he knows that the public could have done perfectly well without. He means that he is printing neither to persuade nor to inform nor yet to express the truth that is in him, but simply to gratify an itch for such notoriety as the careless attention of a few thousand readers may be supposed to give. If I now contrive to escape the consequences of my own axiom it is thanks to you, My Publisher—or Publisher's representative must I say? (You are so very modest, my dear Whitworth, and so exact.) Naturally, by so obliging me you have made me your friend for life. But that was *ex post facto*.

I said just now that when I read Mr. Bennett's "Books and Persons," I was for abandoning a project about which, you will do me the justice of remembering, I was lukewarm from the first. I enjoyed immensely his lively papers and I felt pretty sure that no one would so enjoy mine. Your reader was good enough to point out some reasons, besides the obvious one, why this must be so; and in self-defence I am going to remind you of them. When Mr. Bennett wrote for the *New Age* he was a famous and full-grown author, very much at his ease, very much at his liberty, well aware that if he said what he pleased as he pleased his editor would be only too happy to print it. When I wrote most of the reviews reprinted in this volume I was commencing journalism, and I wrote them for the *Athenæum*.

The *Athenæum*, the editor of which I take this opportunity of thanking for permission to reprint my articles, is a paper, was, at any rate, a paper with ancient and peculiar customs; and of these customs perhaps the most peculiar was that, while allowing its contributors extraordinary liberty in some matters, it sustained what may perhaps be described as a literary policy. Like other venerable institutions, the *Athenæum* had a taste for unwritten law; its policy was adumbrated rather than defined, but few contributors, I believe, were unconscious of its existence. Not one of us, I am sure, would have expressed anything but what he thought and felt, but we all hoped that our thoughts and feelings would not be too dissimilar from those of our presiding genius, Athene the wise, our eponymous goddess; because, if they were, her high-priest, albeit one of the most charming and accomplished people in Fleet Street or thereabouts, stood ready with the inexorable blue pencil to smite once and smite no more. In the matter of expression, too, Her Omniscience was, to my mind, something over-exacting. Concision is an excellent quality in a writer. We all know what Ben Jonson said about Shakespeare and we all agree with him. Still, when, by the shape of one's paragraphs, the balance of one's sentences, and the internal rhythm of one's clauses, one fancies that an article has been raised almost to the perfection of a work of art, it is disappointing to find a line cut out here, two more there, half a dozen missing from the second galley, and from the third a whole paragraph gone for no better reason than that they are not essential to the argument— especially when one is persuaded that they are.

I have said that the editor of the *Athenæum*, in my time, was a charming and accomplished writer; he is also my very good friend and too generous critic, and I should be a wretch if I did not love him. But on the evening when a weekly paper goes to press, when the pages are pouring in, and some one, as likely as not, is waiting at the Café Royal, even the most cultivated and considerate of editors will be an editor. Wherefore I must now plague you and my readers with a word or two in explanation of my method of correction and revision. Re-reading these articles—some of which were written nine or ten years ago—I come on such phrases as "this is a notable achievement," "his equipment is not really strong," and I wonder, of course, what the devil I did say. No doubt it was something definite and particular, for in those days I was a most conscientious writer; but what subtle limitation, what delicately suggested reference, what finely qualifying phrase, what treasure of my critical nonage lies buried beneath this "getting out" formula I cannot now remember. I read the article again and again but I want the courage and energy to read again the book about which it was written. And, if I did, should I recapture precisely what I thought or felt and tried, by means of that lost clause or sentence, not to leave quite unexpressed? The idea is gone, and with it, no doubt, the complete significance of the article. I have botched and cobbled, but at best I have but patched a rent. I hope, however, that I have not spared many of those trusty veterans who, occasionally even in our best weekly and regularly in our morning and evening papers, are expected to do duty for sense.

Wherever the blue pencil or standardized phrase has left too deep a wound or gross a blemish I have had to rewrite. And, as I have rarely succeeded in recovering the original idea, I have had to borrow from my later thought. Of such patching I have been as thrifty as possible: also, I have not attempted to square the opinions and sentiments of early days with my later pronouncements, so, I make no doubt, some very clever readers will have the pleasure of catching me in inconsistency. If they are really clever they will catch me in worse things than that, in puerility for instance, and affectation, to say nothing of blasphemy and sedition. As for consistency, I seem consistently to have cared much for four things—Art, Truth, Liberty and Peace. I was never much in sympathy with my age.

With my youthful style I should not venture to tamper even were I conscious of any important change in my theory of composition or power of expression. And I am not. I write more fluently nowadays and therefore, probably, worse. It cannot be helped. It charms me to notice as I read these essays with what care and conscience they are done. *Magna cum cura atque diligentia scripsit*—they are not far from Latin Grammar days. Precisely on account of these qualities they have suffered much from editorial amendment, and on their account I have been conservative in a matter where another policy would, I dare say, have been more to the taste of some connoisseurs. The matter in question is that of the grand editorial "We." That, as you may suppose, was the person in which Pallas habitually addressed her attentive suppliants; that was the person in which these articles were written; and experiment has shown that to substitute "I," "my," and "mine" for "we," "our," and "ours," destroys invariably the texture of the prose. Whether this early prose of mine was good is not for me to decide; but that it was closely knit is indisputable, and a sensitive critic who cared to tease himself with trifles could discover, I fancy, from stylistic evidence, just which passages have been interpolated.

The articles borrowed from the *Burlington Magazine*, the *Nation*, the *New Statesman*, the *International Journal of Ethics*, and the *Cambridge Magazine*—to the editors of which I herewith tender customary thanks for customary favours—all having appeared over my signature were, of course, all written in the first person singular. Any one who did me the honour of reading my book, "Art," so attentively as now to notice that to its making went certain quarryings from these articles, will have enjoyed it enough, I hope, not to resent being occasionally reminded of it.

And here I might end a tedious letter: but first, if you will bear with me, I should like to say a word on a subject in which both you and I are interested. I have shown so much humility in contrasting these reviews with those of Mr. Bennett that I will permit myself one comment, by no means in disparagement of "Books and Persons," but in the hope that he, or indeed any one who concerns himself with literary criticism, may profit by it. In one respect I do fancy myself a better critic than Mr. Bennett; for though, doubtless, I lack most of those qualities that make his book a positive pleasure to read, I lack also his indiscrimination. Partly, this comes of my not being what he calls himself—"a creative artist," just as it results in my not using that term when I mean "an intelligent person"; but chiefly it is that I am, I believe, almost free from that "provincialism in time"—if I may coin a phrase—which is what is most amiss with Mr. Bennett's critical apparatus. It is a great pity Mr. Bennett should be provincial in any sense, for in the common he is not; on the contrary, he is one who has lived in France, even as Frenchmen live there, without being more than a little shocked. He has read a good many books, both old and new; he is one who cares for literature manifestly: then why does he call Mr. H. G. Wells a great imaginative artist? I will not swear to the epithets—I have not his book by me—but I am sure he is too candid to deny that if he has not used them he has used their equivalents. This much I know he has said—for I made a note when I read the essay—"astounding width of observation, a marvellously true perspective, an extraordinary grasp of the real significance of innumerable phenomena utterly diverse, profound emotional power, dazzling verbal skill." Now, my dear Whitworth, if I were to say that sort of thing about Marivaux you would raise your eyebrows—you know you would. Yet I suppose no competent judge of literature will pretend that the novels of Marivaux—to say nothing of the comedies—are inferior to those of Mr. Wells. Pray read again "Le Paysan Parvenu"—all except the eighth and last part, about which I can't help thinking there is some mystery—and then try "Mr. Britling." But if by Mr. Bennett's standards we are to give Marivaux his due, what is there left to say about Shakespeare?

Provincialism in time is as fatal to judgment as the more notorious sort, and a defective sense of proportion is at the root of both. Consider English novelists of the last hundred years. Who but a fool dare predict confidently for any living Englishman, save Hardy, so much immortality as belongs to Galt's "Annals of the Parish," or Mrs. Oliphant's "Beleagured City"? Now what figure, think you, would a critic cut who besprinkled these writers with such compliments as Mr. Bennett peppers his contemporaries withal? You need not answer. Mr. Bennett is a friend of the firm.

Had Mr. Bennett lost his head about contemporaries who were attempting to solve new artistic problems I could understand it. Young writers wax over-enthusiastic about Laforgue and Charles-Louis Philippe—both of whom, by the way, died some years ago—and are not much to blame on that account; neither should I have the least difficulty in forgiving myself were it to turn out—as it will not—that I had said too much in praise of Matisse or Picasso. The artist who even appears to have discovered or rediscovered an instrument of expression or to have extended by one semitone the gamut of æsthetic experience is bound to turn the best heads of his age. Were it possible to overrate Cézanne, not to do so would be a mark of insensibility. I was never much impressed by those superior persons of an earlier age who from the first saw through Wagner; there was a time when to dislike Wagner was, in ninety-nine cases out of a hundred, a sign not of superiority but of stupidity. The artists, however, whom Mr. Bennett belauds so uncritically, are not of this sort. In my judgment, Mr. Wells, Mr. George Moore, and the late Sir John Galsworthy are not artists at all: be that as it may, past question they are artistically conventional and thoroughly in the tradition of British fiction. Of course they write of motor-cars and telephones where an older generation wrote of railway-trains and telegrams, and of the *deuxièmes*, *troisièmes* or *quatre-vingt-dixièmes* where their grandmothers wrote of *les premiers amours*; also, they can refer to the Almighty in the third person without bursting into capitals. But in this there is no more artistic novelty than there would be in a picture of an aeroplane painted in the manner of Ingres. Neither is there any discredit; very much the same might be said of our three best living novelists—Hardy, Conrad, and Virginia Woolf, all of whom are more or less traditional, as is Anatole France, perhaps the best novelist alive. A first-rate unconventional work of art is not a straw better than a conventional one, and to become slightly light-headed about either is not only permissible but seemly. Nevertheless, to go silly over a mediocre innovation is far more excusable than to be taken in by its equivalent in a familiar style. While to rave about Messrs. Wells, Moore and Galsworthy seems to me shocking. Surely there can be no difficulty about treating these writers as ordinary citizens of the Republic of Letters—a state, let us try to remember, that not only extends in space beyond the horizons of Tooting but in time beyond the Edwardian and even the Victorian era.

A critic, I submit, should judge a work of art, not in relation to the age and circumstances in which it was produced, but by an absolute standard based on the whole *corpus* of that art to which the particular work belongs. We do not want to hear how good "Tono-Bungay" seems by comparison with Mrs. Ward's last production. Marvellous, no doubt: so, no doubt, are Mrs. Ward's intellectual gifts by comparison with those of a walrus. But we want to have Mrs. Ward judged as a specimen of Humanity and "Tono-Bungay" as a specimen of Literature. It must be tried by the standards we try "Tristram Shandy" and "La Princesse de Clèves" by. How, then, does it stand? With "Liaisons Dangereuses"? Hardly. Well, is it of the class of "Evelina" or of "Adolphe," or of "Consuelo" even? Mr. Bennett can be as sharp as a special constable with Thackeray: is it as good as "Pendennis"? And, unless it be infinitely better, what sense is there in despising Thackeray and extolling Mr. Wells? Pray, Mr. Bennett, how good is this book? Let us see; I think I have a note on the subject: "his scientific romances" are "on the plane of epic poetry" and "in 'Tono-Bungay' he has achieved the same feat, magnified by ten—or a hundred"; "there are passages toward the close of the book which may fitly be compared with the lyrical freedoms of no matter what epic, and which display an unsurpassable dexterity of hand." And now what are we to say of "Manon Lescaut"? That it is a million times better than Milton and knocks spots off Homer? But all this though distressing is not conclusive; it proves provinciality but it proves nothing worse. Mr. Bennett may really have been thinking all the time of "Robert Elsmere" and "The Epic of Hades." About another of his favourites, however, he is more precise: "I re-read 'A Man of Property,'" he says, "immediately after re-reading Dostoievsky's 'Crime and Punishment,' and immediately before re-reading Björnson's 'Arne.' It ranks well with these European masterpieces." I repeat that in one respect I am a better critic than Mr. Bennett.

This question of criticism fascinates me. It interests Mr. Bennett, too, and he has written several competent and surprisingly confident articles on the subject. I could almost wish to discuss one of them with him. I would help him to understand Coleridge and tell him about Dryden's essays and Johnson's "Lives of the Poets," and I would assure him, too, it was not I who wrote that unfortunate review of Conrad that gets such an exemplary drubbing at his hands for its self-complacent imbecility. He ought to know that, or he will think that I speak out of malice. He says that England has need of a literary critic. I agree. And I agree that this critic must not be of that professorial breed with which he deals so faithfully, not one who will date you every line in Shakespeare on internal evidence and then obligingly pronounce Sir Arthur Conan Doyle our greatest living writer. He will need the intelligence, the first-hand views, the open mind, the genuine taste for books, the respect for art and irreverence for persons of Mr. Bennett himself; and, as I have hinted, he will need one or two qualities for which Mr. Bennett is not so well off. He must be a resolute critic of literature and not an authority on current reputations; he must have enough natural taste to recognize a work of art in odd company, new clothes, or fancy dress; he must be the sort of person who would have seen at a glance that Kipling or Paul Bourget was not the real thing; he must be a scholar and a man of the intellectual world: and he must be as incapable of calling Mr. George Moore "a great artist" or speaking of "a first-rate beautiful thing" by that gentleman as Mr. Bennett is of eating peas with his knife.

The critic of our dreams—Mr. Bennett's and mine—has yet to be found. You will not imagine, surely, that I am putting myself forward as a candidate? Here you will find very few of the virtues and some, I suspect, of the critical vices to which I have alluded in this letter. But you need not fear, my dear Whitworth, that I am now going to tax your good nature by an elaborate defence of these essentially insignificant papers. They are an odd lot, and I think there are but two—the two last—that I am not a little ashamed of reprinting. Clearly, were I now to write on the same themes I should have something very different to say and should say it differently. Honestly, I believe these things are worth reading; I can say no more for them and I shall hold him generous who says as much. But the pleasure I shall derive from seeing them printed and off my hands will be as great almost as that which I felt when, four years ago, you, or your firm rather, did me the honour of publishing a book to which I attached, and continue to attach, a good deal of importance. Here I am harvesting my wild oats; and that deed done, I expect to feel what a regular but rather humdrum sinner must feel as he returns from Confession. Quit of my past, I shall be ready to turn over a new leaf. I shall be able, if I please, to approach life from a new angle and try my luck in unexplored countries, so far, that is, as the European situation permits.

C. B.

February 1918.

- 7 -

MONTAIGNE IN FACSIMILE[1]

Athenæum Jan. 1913

Let it be understood at once that the appearance of this magnificent work is a bibliophilic rather than a literary event. The literary event was the publication by M. Fortunat Strowski, in 1909, of "L'Edition Municipale," an exact transcription of that annotated copy of the 1588 quarto known to fame as "L'Exemplaire de Bordeaux." What the same eminent scholar gives us now is a reproduction in phototype of "L'Exemplaire." Any one, therefore, who goes to these volumes in search of literary discoveries is foredoomed to disappointment. Indeed, the same might have been said of "L'Edition Municipale"; for the "Motheau et Jouaust" edition, reprinted by MM. Flammarion in their "Bibliothèque classique," was complete enough to satisfy all but the most meticulous scholars, while for general literary purposes the edition published in 1595, three years after the author's death, by his niece, Mlle. de Gournay, is sufficient and adequate.

Though five editions of the "Essais" were printed during their author's life—1580 and 1582 at Bordeaux, 1584 (probably) and 1587 at Paris, 1588 at Bordeaux—to critics in search of dramatic spiritual changes a comparative study will afford but meagre sport. To be sure, the editions of '84 and '87 were nothing more than what we should now call reprints; but the edition of 1588, of which "L'Exemplaire de Bordeaux" is a copy, represents so thorough an overhauling and so generous an enlarging of the old book that some have been tempted to reckon it a new one. Yet, though it garners the fruit of eight fertile years of travel and public service, it reveals no startling change in the outlook, nor in what is more important, the insight, of its author. We need feel no surprise. Had Montaigne been the sort of man whose views and sentiments are profoundly affected by travel or office, he would not have been the object of that cult of which the three volumes before us are the latest, and perhaps the most significant, monument. That is a peculiar man whose crossings and dottings and deletions are judged worthy of photographic record by the authorities of a great industrial city.

Montaigne was thoroughly normal, not to say commonplace, in his ability to pass through foreign countries without suffering anything so alarming as a conversion. He left home on his travels in Germany, Switzerland, and Italy, a learned and extremely intelligent man of affairs, who had taken, rather late in life perhaps, to playing the part of a French country gentleman; he returned with a store of acute observations and pleasant anecdotes, a little older, a little mellower, otherwise unchanged. Of those magically expanded views, those sudden yawnings of sympathetic depths, that nowadays every one may count on winning, if not by a week in Brittany, at any rate by a month in Manitoba, we find scarcely a trace. In the sixteenth century that sort of thing was unusual. Even in those days there were people of extraordinary sensibility for whom life was a succession of miracles, who with difficulty recognized themselves from year to year, to whom going abroad was an emotional adventure, a supreme revelation: but of these Montaigne was not one. Him, like some others, change seems merely to have confirmed in his native predispositions and prejudices. As he grew older he grew vainer, rather more garrulous, fonder of his favourite authors, and a little less open-minded; and his travels were nothing more than a long and agreeable stage on the longest journey. There are people for whom travel provides nothing but supplementary evidence in a cause that has already been judged. Those who can find nothing good at home will smack their lips over the sourest wines abroad; and "Old Meynell" need not have left his garden to arrive at that conclusion commended by Dr. Johnson: "For anything I see, foreigners are fools." Montaigne was not of these, either; too normal to be above patriotism, he was too proud and too intelligent to be blindly patriotic.

Montaigne was the ideal man-in-the-street. We do not mean that he was typical; but if there are men-in-the-street in heaven, they will resemble Montaigne. And though we rank a third-rate saint or artist a great deal higher than a first-rate good fellow, we recognize that there is something about any kind of perfection that dazzles even those who are most alive to its essential inferiority. Montaigne is the exemplar of good feeling and good sense; in him we see those qualities chatting on terms of familiarity with genius and inspiration. He held the views that all sensible people would hold if only all were as intelligent and benevolent as they honestly believe themselves to be; he expressed them in a form appropriate to, and therefore limited by, his subject, but, within those limits, perfect.

The form in which Montaigne expressed himself was new to French literature. In the sixteenth century there was a recognized literary style based on the Latin period. Sentences were long, sonorous, and circuitous. It was a language well suited to those who followed the profession of letters, but unserviceable to one who would communicate his thoughts and feelings to others. Montaigne was not a professional author; he was a country gentleman with something of his own to say. The literature of the professionals was an ingenious and abstract superstructure built up over an idea or an emotion. Montaigne wished to set down the original thought or feeling as it sprang, hot, from the mind; and, as original thoughts and feelings present themselves always with the force of sensations, he gave them the forms of sensations—that is to say, he wrote in images. He expressed his philosophy of good sense in short, hard, coloured sentences, keeping them as close as possible to the naked thoughts they conveyed. That in print they appear as long as those of his contemporaries is a mere accident of typography; for almost every semicolon in the "Essais" one may substitute a full stop: very rarely is the long sentence in Montaigne a period.

Like most sensible men, Montaigne had an unreasonable fondness for reason; unlike most, he possessed an intellect that showed him the final consequences of his fancy. Not only have we no sufficient reason for believing that we know anything, we have none for affirming that we know nothing. By sheer reasonableness we are reduced to a state of pure Pyrrhonism, where, like the poor donkey, we must die of starvation midway between two equally large and equally appetizing bundles of hay. An affectation of superior ignorance has been a favourite literary device from the days of the Preacher to those of Anatole France. Montaigne loves to tease and confound us with a "Que sçay-ie," he has the common literary taste for humiliating unsympathetic readers; but he has also a taste for honesty not so common, even in literature. Doubt is a mark of good sense: honest doubt is a mark of genius almost. In his reflective moments the reasonable man inclines to believe that reason can prove nothing—except what he believes. How fearlessly did those nineteenth-century apostles of Reason make havoc in the parlours of meek curates and spinsters, thundering against the altogether insufficient grounds on which were accepted the surprising adventures of Noah and his Ark! But when they were told that Reason was as unfriendly to their moral code and the methods of science as to the Book of Genesis, they clapped her in jail without more ado. Reason affords no solid grounds for holding a good world better than a bad, and the sacred law of cause and effect itself admits of no logical demonstration. "Prison or the Mad House," cried the men of good sense; Montaigne was more thorough—"Tolerance," said he.

Like the man-in-the-street, Montaigne found refuge from reason in conviction. Until we have formulated a proposition reason has no excuse for interference; and emotional convictions precede intellectual propositions. Only, as we have no means of judging between convictions, we must remember that the firm and disinterested convictions of others are as respectable as our own: again we must tolerate. To credit Montaigne with that sublime liberality which is summed up in the most sublime of all Christian aphorisms—"Judge not, and thou shalt not be judged"—would be absurd. Montaigne was a Pagan, and his high conception of tolerance and humanity was derived entirely from the great pagan philosophers. Of them he was a profound and sincere disciple, so it is not surprising that his ideas were far in advance of those of his age, and of ours. For instance, he hated brutality. Both his own nature and that fine Athenian humanity which by study he had made his own were revolted by barbarous punishments. That there may be men too vile to live seemed to him, doubtless, a tenable opinion—he could forget all about the fallibility of human judgments—but "Quant à moy," he says, "en la iustice mesme, tout ce qui est au delà de la mort simple, me semble pure cruauté." To hurt others for our own good is not, he dimly perceived, to cut a very magnanimous figure. To call it hurting them for their own, he would have thought damnable; but that piece of hypocrisy is the invention of a more enlightened age. Torture he abhorred. Assuredly Montaigne would have been more at home in the streets of Periclean Athens than in those of sixteenth-century Bordeaux or twentieth-century London.

Nothing illustrates better Montaigne's essential paganism than his passionate admiration for magnanimity. That was the virtue he loved. High courage and fortitude, dignity, patience, and generosity—these are qualities, examples of which never fail to strike a spark of enthusiasm from his calm nature. He is never tired of extolling the constancy of Socrates and Cato, the courage of Cæsar, the generosity of Alexander, the great and grandiose actions of the heroes of antiquity. Indeed, this admiration for courage and dignity so transports him that once, at any rate, he surpasses most pagan philosophers, and joins hands with the latest and most Christian of Christian moralists:

> "A quoy faire nous allons nous gendarmant par ces efforts de la science? Regardons à terre, les pauvres gens que nous y voyons espandus, la teste panchante apres leur besongne: qui ne sçavent ny Aristote ny Caton, ny exemple ny precepte. De ceux-là, tire Nature tous les iours, des effects de constance et de patience, plus purs et plus roides, que ne sont ceux que nous estudions si curieusement en l'escole. Combien en vois ie ordinairement, qui mescognoissent la pauvreté: combien qui desirent la mort, ou qui la passent sans alarme et sans affliction? Celui là qui fouit mon iardin, il a ce matin enterré son pere ou son fils. Les noms mesme, dequoy ils appellent les maladies, en addoucissent et amollissent l'aspreté. La phthysie, c'est la toux pour eux: la dysenterie, devoyment d'estomach: un pleuresis, c'est un morfondement: et selon qu'ils les nomment doucement, ils les supportent aussi. Elles sont bien griefves, quand elles

rompent leur travail ordinaire: ils ne s'allitent que pour mourir."

This passage is exceptional; it is not the less sincere. Of its sincerity no one who reads and feels can doubt. But generally the instances of eximious virtue are what Montaigne delights to honour. Nothing in him is more lovable than this passionate hero-worship; and what quality is more lovable or more common in the ordinary man?

"Le plus sage des Français," Sainte-Beuve called him; the judgment is typical of the critic and his age. We need not stay to quarrel with it. We can hold that there is a higher wisdom than the quest of golden mediocrity without disparaging either Horace or his disciple. If the man-in-the-street be one who approaches the obvious in the spirit of a pioneer, we must admit that Montaigne rises superior to his class, for he not only explored that country, but possessed and cultivated it too, and forced it to yield an ampler harvest of good sense and humanity than any other husbandman before or since. France has ever been rich, and is as rich as ever, in men who have known how to sacrifice the shadow to the substance; in fanatics who have pursued without pause or divagation dreams of impossible Utopias and unattainable good; in idealists who have joyfully given all to love, to art, to religion, and to logic. It is not inappropriate, therefore, that France should have produced in an age of turmoil and terrible madness the man who exalted the cult of moderation to the heights of sublime philosophy.

FOOTNOTE:

[1] "Reproduction en Phototypie de l'Exemplaire, avec Notes manuscrites marginales, des Essais de Montaigne appartenant à la Ville de Bordeaux." Publiée, avec une Introduction, par Fortunat Strowski. 3 vols. (Paris, Hachette.)

IBSEN[2]

Athenæum June 1912

Was it chance made Mr. Ellis Roberts mention Cézanne on the fourth page of a book about Ibsen? One cannot think so. Similarities in the work and circumstances of the two men can hardly have escaped him. Born within a dozen years of each other (Ibsen was born in 1828), both matured in a period when the professions of writing and painting were laboriously cultivated at the expense of art. Each, unguided except by his own sense of dissatisfaction with his surroundings, found a way through the sloughs of romance and the deserts of realism, to the high country beyond them. Both sought and both found the same thing—the thing above literature and painting, the stuff out of which great literature and painting are made.

The Romantics and Realists were like people coming to cuffs about which is the more important thing in an orange, the history of Spain or the number of pips. The instinct of the romantic, invited to say what he felt about anything, was to recall its associations. A rose made him think of quaint gardens and gracious ladies and Edmund Waller and sundials, and a thousand pleasant things that, at one time or another, had befallen him or some one else. A rose touched life at a hundred pretty points. A rose was interesting because it had a past. On this the realist's comment was "Mush!" or words to that effect. In like predicament, he would give a detailed account of the properties of *Rosa setigera*, not forgetting to mention the urn-shaped calyx-tube, the five imbricated lobes, or the open corolla of five obovate petals. To an Ibsen or a Cézanne one account would appear as irrelevant as the other, since both omitted the thing that mattered, what philosophers used to call "the thing in itself," what now they would call "the essential reality":

> SOLNESS. ... Do you read much?
>
> HILDA. No, never! I have given it up. For it all seems so irrelevant.
>
> SOLNESS. That is just my feeling.

It was just what the books left out that Ibsen wanted to express.

He soon worked through the romantic tradition. It hampered him long enough to prevent *Peer Gynt* from becoming a great poem; after that he found himself on the threshold of a world where everything mattered too much in itself for its associations to be of consequence. Attempting to analyse Ibsen's characters used to be a pastime for fools; to-day, we all know that they come from that world where everything has been reduced to an essence that defies analysis. There Ibsen was never so completely at home as Cézanne; he lacked the imagination by which alone one arrives and remains in the world of reality. His vision was more uncertain and so his faith was weaker. He was a less ferociously sincere artist. When vision began to fail he took refuge in a catalogue of facts or in unconvincing symbolism: Cézanne tossed his picture into a bush. Perhaps that is why a new generation, hungry for great contemporary art, turns more hopefully to painting than to literature.

Thirty years ago it would have been misleading to say, what is undoubtedly true, that it is as an artist that Ibsen is great. To call a man a good artist came to much the same thing as calling him a good ping-pong player: it implied that he was proficient in his own business; it did not imply that he was a great man who affected life greatly. Therefore many people who understood Ibsen and were moved by his plays preferred to call him a political thinker or a social reformer; while their enemies, the æsthetes, were very willing to call him a great artist, since by doing so they excused themselves from paying the least attention to anything that he said. Ibsen was a reformer in the sense that all great artists are reformers; it is impossible to speak of reality without criticizing civilization. In the same way he was a politician; it is impossible to care passionately about art without caring about the fate of mankind. But Mr. Roberts is certainly right in holding that to appreciate Ibsen we must consider him as an artist.

Ibsen approached humanity in the spirit of an artist. He sought that essential thing in men and women by which we should know them if the devil came one night and stole away their bodies; we may call it character if we choose. He imagined situations in which character would be revealed clearly. The subjects of his plays are often "problems," because he was interested in people who only when "problems" arise are seen to be essentially different from one another, or, indeed, from the furniture with which they live. There is no reason to suppose that Ibsen had any love for "problems" as such; and we are tempted to believe that some modern "problems" are nothing more than situations from Ibsen's plays. Ibsen's method is the true artist's method. The realist writing about people tends to give an inventory of personal peculiarities, and a faithful report of all that is said and done. The romantic hopes, somehow, to "create an atmosphere" by suggesting what he once felt for something not altogether unlike the matter in hand. Ibsen sets himself to discover the halfpennyworth of significance in all this intolerable deal of irrelevance. Which is the word, which the gesture, that, springing directly from the depths of one character, penetrates to the depths of another? What is the true cause of this hubbub of inconsequent words and contradictory actions? Nothing less remote than the true cause will serve, nothing else is firmly rooted in reality. Is that man expressing what he feels or is he paying out what he thinks he is expected to feel? Have I pushed simplification as far as it will go? Are there no trappings, no overtones, nothing but what is essential to express my vision of reality? And, above all, is my vision absolutely sharp and sure? These were the questions Ibsen had to answer. When he succeeded he was a great artist, not, as Mr. Roberts suggests, in the manner of Shakespeare, but in the manner of Æschylus.

There is no more obvious proof of the greatness of Ibsen's art than the perfection of its form. To assert that fine form always enfolds fine thought and feeling would imply a knowledge of literature to which it would be effrontery in a critic to pretend. He may be allowed, however, to advise any one who is ready with an instance of great form enclosing a void to verify his impressions: it was thus that one critic at any rate came to appreciate Goldoni and Alfieri. Be that as it may, this is certain: a perfectly conceived idea never fails to express itself in perfect form. Ibsen did not shirk the labour of making his conceptions as hard, and definite, and self-supporting as possible. No matter how autobiographical some of his best plays may be, he is too good an artist to allow them to lean on his personal experience; they have to stand firmly on their own feet. Ibsen, therefore, worked his conceptions to such a degree of hardness and self-consistency that he could detach them from himself and study them impersonally. That is why his plays are models of form. And if there be an Academy of Letters that takes its duties seriously, *Rosmersholm* and *Ghosts* are, we presume, in the hands of every young person within its sphere of influence. The students are shown, we hope, that Ibsen's form is superb, not because Ibsen paid any particular attention to the precepts of Aristotle, but because, like Sophocles, who had the misfortune to predecease the Stagirite, he knew precisely what he wanted to say, and addressed himself exclusively to the task of saying it. To achieve great form is needed neither science nor tradition, but intense feeling, vigorous thinking, and imagination. Formlessness is not a sign of spirited revolt against superstition; it is a mere indication of muddleheadedness.

The subject-matter of Ibsen's plays is reality; unfortunately, his imagination was not always strong enough to keep a sure hold on it. When the vision faded he took refuge in symbolism or literality. There was a commonplace background to his mind, of which we see too much in such plays as *An Enemy of the People* and *Pillars of Society*. It is this commonplace and rather suburban quality that tempts us occasionally to explain Ibsen's popularity by the fact that he represented the revolt of the supremely unimportant, of whom there happen to be quite a number in the world. With the symbolism of *The Master-Builder* no fault can be found. It is a legitimate and effective means of expressing a sense of reality. The theme is never lost. The artist who sacrifices his human relations, but dare not give all, dare not give his vanity or his life to the ideal, moves steadily to his inevitable doom. Whether he move in the form of Halvard Solness, the cowardly architect of genius, fearless of ideas but fearful of action, or in the form of the symbolical master-builder, the artist who tries to have the best of both worlds, matters not a straw. The medium of expression changes, but the theme is constant: the conception is whole. That is more than can be said of *The Lady from the Sea*, where the symbolism comes perilously near padding; or of *When We Dead Awaken*, where it often expresses nothing relevant, merely standing picturesquely for commonplaces, and filling gaps.

To read one of Ibsen's great plays is always thrilling; to read one for the first time is an event. If a savage who took locomotives and motor-cars for granted, as inexplicable creatures of whim and fancy, suddenly were shown, not by vague adumbration, but by straightforward exposition, that they were expressions of intelligible laws controlled by comprehensible machinery, he could not be more amazed than was the nineteenth century by Ibsen. For Ibsen took nothing for granted. He saw little on the surface of life that corresponded with reality; but he did not cease to believe in reality. That was where he differed both from the Philistines and from the elect. He saw that the universe was something very different from what it was generally supposed to be: he saw the futility of popular morals and popular metaphysics; but he neither swallowed the conventions nor threw up his hands in despair, declaring the whole thing to be an idiotic farce. He knew that truth and goodness had nothing to do with law and custom; but he never doubted that there were such things; and he went beneath the surface to find them. It was Ibsen's revelation of a new world, in which moral values were real and convincing, that thrilled the nineteenth century, and thrills us yet. Can any one read sedately that scene in *Ghosts* in which Mrs. Alving shows with bewildering simplicity that, however respectable the Pastor's morality may be, it is pure wickedness?

> PASTOR MANDERS. You call it "cowardice" to do your plain duty? Have you forgotten that a son ought to love and honour his father and mother?

> MRS. ALVING. Do not let us talk in such general terms. Let us ask: Ought Oswald to love and honour Chamberlain Alving?

> MANDERS. Is there no voice in your mother's heart that forbids you to destroy your son's ideals?

MRS. ALVING. But what about the truth?

MANDERS. But what about the ideals?

MRS. ALVING. Oh—ideals, ideals! If only I were not such a coward!

Ibsen's social and political ideas follow necessarily from the nature of his art. He knew too much about the depths of character to suppose that people could be improved from without. He agreed with our grandmothers that what men need are new hearts. It is good feeling that makes good men, and the sole check on bad feeling is conscience. Laws, customs, and social conventions he regarded as ineffectual means to good. There is no virtue in one who is restrained from evil by fear. He went further: he regarded external restraints as means to bad, since they come between a man and his conscience and blunt the moral sense. "So long as I keep to the rules," says the smug citizen, "I am of the righteous." Ibsen loathed the State, with its negative virtues, its mean standards, its mediocrity, and its spiritual squalor. He was a passionate individualist.

Perhaps no one has seen more clearly that the State, at its best, stands for nothing better than the lowest common factor of the human mind. What else can it stand for? State ideals must be ideals that are not beyond the intellect and imagination of "the average citizen"; also, since average minds are not pervious to reason, the reasoning of statesmen must be rhetoric. State morals—law and custom that is to say—are nothing more than excuses for not bothering about conscience. But Ibsen, being an artist, knew that he who would save his soul must do what he feels to be right, not what is said to be so. Feeling is the only guide, and the man who does what he feels to be wrong does wrong, whatever the State may say.

The plain, though by no means frank, determination of society to suppress the individual conscience lest it should clash with the interests of the community seems positively to have shocked him. To be fine, he believed, men must think and feel for themselves and live by their own sense of truth and beauty, not by collective wisdom or reach-me-down ideals.

> "What sort of truths do the majority rally round? Truths so stricken in years that they are sinking into decrepitude. When a truth is so old as that, gentlemen, it's in a fair way to become a lie (*Laughter and jeers*)."

How could Ibsen help being something of a politician? He seems really to have wished his fellow-creatures to be fine, and to have been angry with them because they wished to be nothing of the sort. He did not understand that this passionate individualism, this sense of personal responsibility, this claim to private judgment, is what no modern State, be it democratic, bureaucratic or autocratic, can tolerate. Men long for the ease and assurance of conformity and so soon as they are sufficiently organized enforce it. Truth is the enemy—*écrasez l'infâme!* Poor, silly old Stockmann in *An Enemy of the People* blurts it out, blurts out that the water-supply is contaminated and his native health-resort no better than a death-trap, for no better reason than that he feels it is what he ought to do. He fails to consider the feelings and, what is even more important, the financial interests of his neighbours, and the neighbours make short work of him, as they generally do of people who think and feel and act for themselves—of saints and artists in fact. Thus it comes about that the prophets are stoned and the best plays censored, while people such as Ibsen loathe the State with its herd-instincts, now decently baptized however, and known as Morality and Idealism.

Whether Ibsen was in the right is not for a reviewer to decide. Mr. Roberts has strong views on the subject, which he is at no pains to conceal. For this we are far from blaming him. Indeed, we feel that the personal note imported by the author's intellectual bias gives some flavour to a book which, owing to the complete absence of charm or distinction, would be otherwise insipid. It is a competent, but woefully uninspiring, piece of work. Above all things, Mr. Roberts lacks humour—a quality indispensable in a writer on Ibsen. For Ibsen, like other men of genius, is slightly ridiculous. Undeniably, there is something comic about the picture of the Norwegian dramatist, spectacled and frock-coated, "looking," Mr. Archer tells us, "like a distinguished diplomat," at work amongst the orange-groves of Sorrento on *Ghosts*.

> "Ibsen was keenly sensitive to place, and if we would get the utmost feeling out of his plays we must remember how large a part was played by fortunate or unfortunate position and circumstances in contributing to the wonderful 'atmosphere' of the dramas."

That is what Mr. Roberts thinks. A sense of humour would also have saved him from the one black note of sentimentality in the book:

> "Ellida might be Solveig analysed—but analysed with how loving a touch, how unerring a kindness; it is as if a great surgeon were operating on a woman he loved."

Such things, we had imagined, could only be written by members of the Académie française.

FOOTNOTE:

[2] "Henrik Ibsen: a Critical Study." By R. Ellis Roberts. (Secker.)

MISS COLERIDGE[3]

Athenæum July 1910

The greatest art is, in a sense, impersonal. We have no biographies of Homer and Sophocles, nor do we need them. Of Milton and Keats we know something; yet, knowing nothing, should we enjoy their work the less? It is not for what it reveals of Milton that we prize "Paradise Lost"; the "Grecian Urn" lives independent of its author and his circumstances, a work of art, complete in itself.

Precisely opposite is the case of Miss Mary Coleridge's poems: they, when in 1908 Mr. Elkin Mathews produced a more or less complete edition, excited us, not because, as verse, they were particularly good, but because they discovered, or seemed to discover, an attractive character. Indeed, Miss Coleridge's art was anything but exciting: her diction was not beautiful, her rhythms pleased the ear but moderately, one looked in vain for that magic of expression which transmutes thought and feeling into poetry. But if the expression wanted magic, that which was expressed seemed an enchantment almost. The gentle spirit, with its vein of tender pessimism, in puzzled revolt against the wrongness and cruelty of a shadowy world, the brooding thought too whimsical to be bitter, the fancy too refined to be boisterously merry—all these conspired to fascinate us as we came to perceive and appreciate them beneath the rather stiff little verses. To read Miss Coleridge's poems was to make acquaintance with a charming and delicate soul that wished to be understood and was willing to be intimate. Life astonished her, and her comments on life are her poems. They are often mystical, not to say obscure; and the obscurity, as a rule, is caused by vagueness rather than profundity, by the fact that she hardly knows herself what she feels, or thinks, or believes. But from so gracious a spirit one accepts without demur that which from another would not have passed unchallenged. Miss Coleridge bewitched us with her personality; we knew that her poems were slight, we felt that they revealed a part of her only, we had suspicions, but we held our peace. Had we turned to her novels, in spite of the brilliancy of one of them—"The King with Two Faces"—our suspicions would have been strengthened. But we did not turn; or if we did, they forced us into no questioning mood. It was left for this tell-tale volume of "Gathered Leaves" to press the question insistently, and to answer it. The spell is broken. We know now both why the poems are good and why they are not better.

No one will blame Miss Sichel for setting the truth before all things: clearly, by publishing these stories and essays she supplies an opportunity of correcting a too flattering estimate; but, foreseeing, no doubt, that we shall avail ourselves of it, she supplies also a memoir of fifty pages on which our final estimate is to be based. That this memoir is a competent piece of work need hardly be said. Miss Sichel's competence is notorious; as an efficient biographer her reputation is secure. Not every subject, however, is suited to her pen. Miss Coleridge did not develop along conventional lines; in fact, she differed so disconcertingly from the type with which we have grown agreeably familiar in the "English Men of Letters" series, that, without violence, she could never have been fitted into the traditional mould. Her biographer has done the work thoroughly, but she is a thought heavy in the hand; she is too literary, not to say professional; she is definite at all costs. She has "restored" Miss Coleridge as a German archæologist might restore a Tanagra figure. Indeterminate lines have been ruthlessly rectified and asymmetry has grown symmetrical. Though we do not suggest that she misunderstood her friend, we are sure that the lady exhibited in the memoir is not the lady who reveals herself in the poems.

Of the author of the poems we catch a glimpse in the fragments of letters and diaries which form the penultimate section of the volume. But here, again, we find cause for discontent. If private reasons forbade fullness, was it wise to print scraps? Why tantalize us? In the letters we should, perhaps, have recaptured the lady we have lost in the essays and stories; but these fragments, though suggestive, are too slight to be consolatory: besides, Miss Coleridge was no coiner of aphorisms and epigrams who could give her meaning in a handful of sentences. Here is the first "detached thought" in the book:

> "'Whom the gods love die young' and whom they hate die old, but whom they honour, these they take up to their eternal habitations in the ripe summer time of existence."

One wonders how it came there.

The suspicions which this volume helps to confirm, the melancholy guesses it answers, are that Miss Coleridge, with all her imagination, had not the constructive imagination of an artist, and that, in spite of her gaiety and spirits, fundamentally she was feeble. The imagination of an artist, if we may be allowed a seeming paradox, works logically. Not fortuitously, but by some mysterious necessity, does one vision follow another. There is a rational, if unconscious, order in the pageantry of images; there is an inevitableness in their succession closely allied to the logical necessity by which one idea follows another in a well-reasoned argument. In Miss

Coleridge's mind images arranged themselves in no progressive order; one bears no particular relationship to another; they are disconnected, sporadic. Great imagination is architectural; it sets fancy upon fancy until it has composed a splendid and intelligible whole—a valid castle in the air. Miss Coleridge could not build; ideas broke in her mind in showers of whims, and lay where they fell at haphazard; she has bequeathed no castles, but a garden strewn with quaint figures, where every thought is tagged with gay conceits. Her short poems are often successful because she could pick at choice a thought or fancy and twist it into a stanza; but when she attempted a tale or an essay she gathered a handful of incongruous oddments and made of them a patchwork.

This first defect was, we conjecture, a consequence of that other and more fundamental flaw to which we have already drawn attention. If Miss Coleridge's artificers played truant, it was because she lacked strength to keep them at their task. For an indolent and lawless imagination force of character is the only whip, force of intellect the only guide. Miss Coleridge was deficient in both respects, and so her fancy sat playing with chips and pebbles, making mud-pies when it should have been making palaces.

Miss Coleridge never created a real work of art because she could not grasp emotions, or, if she grasped, failed to hold them. Perhaps she was too much of a Victorian lady to do more than express the culture of an imperfect age imperfectly. At any rate, it is clear that a shrinking fastidiousness excluded from her world much of the raw material from which great art is made. Stray reflections on Greek life and thought, though in themselves trivial, are interesting for what they betray of a state of mind familiar and always slightly distressing to people who take art seriously. She was a fair scholar Miss Sichel tells us; certainly she studied under an excellent master—the author of "Ionica"; yet she could say of the "Bacchæ": "The Hallelujah Lasses get drunk on the wine of the spirit, not the wine of the grape"; and of the "Medea":

> "Medea is thoroughly *fin de siècle*; says she would rather go into battle three times than have a baby once, pitches into men like anything. But there's too much Whitechapel about her. How are you to be seriously interested in a woman who has murdered her mother and boiled her father-in-law before the play begins?"

What is this but the shy jauntiness, the elaborate understatement, of something small in the presence of something great? That uneasy titter, caught from time to time as one turns Miss Coleridge's pages, we seem to have heard before in the Arena chapel or at the end of a Bach fugue. It is the comment of sophisticated refinement that can neither sit still nor launch out into rapturous, but ill-bred, ecstasies, of the weakling who takes refuge in slang or jocularity for fear of becoming natural and being thought ridiculous. Miss Coleridge stood for Kensington and Culture, so she smiled and shrugged her shoulders at Medea, and called the Bacchæ "Hallelujah Lasses." She and Kensington admired Greek literature and art, of course, with enthusiasm tempered by taste; but the "glory that was Greece," the merciless honesty and riotous passions, the adventurous thought and feeling, were meat too strong for a society whose happiness depended on gazing at one half of life with closed eyes and swallowing the other in sugar-coated pills.

So we shall not turn again to "Gathered Leaves," though we shall sometimes read the poems. Henceforth, they will conjure up a less elusive figure. They will show us a pensive lady, rather well dressed in the fashion of five-and-twenty years ago, who sits in a Morris drawing-room, the white walls of which are spotted with Pre-Raphaelite pictures, and muses on what her surroundings represent. She is intelligent and graceful; witty in season, fantastic in measure. Her mind is ruffled by the perplexities appropriate to her age and state; she searches Canon Dixon's latest poem for light on Holman Hunt's last picture. Her life is an exquisite preoccupation with the surface of truth and the heart of unreality. Her poems suggest once more the atmosphere of an age already dead and half-forgotten; of Sunday afternoons in large rooms with long blinds, behind which men yawn and cultivated women are earnest and playful; of a world in which people must pretend courageously that life is very important for fear of discovering that it hardly signifies. It is a strange world, faded, friendly, urbane, and, we are happy to think, already infinitely remote.

FOOTNOTE:

[3] "Gathered Leaves from the Prose of Mary E. Coleridge." With a Memoir by Edith Sichel. (Constable and Co.)

This review, when first published, gave pain, I know; it gave pain to friends of Miss Coleridge and to friends of Miss Sichel and to many of the charming people who were friends of both. The pain, of course, I regret; but I cannot say that I regret the article. The criticism still seems to me fair, and I know that it was honest: nevertheless, were Miss Sichel alive, I should not care to reprint it. But that able and friendly lady is now dead, and her eulogy has been pronounced by those who knew her best and could best appreciate her. I, of course, have criticized her only in her public character, as a writer, and in so doing have transgressed no law that I, at any rate, can respect. As Voltaire says, "On doit des égards aux vivants; on ne doit aux morts que la vérité." To the living, perhaps, I have not always been as civil as could have been desired; but of the dead I have told no lies that I am aware of.

PEACOCK[4]

I

Athenæum Feb. 1911

In the first place, were these plays worth publishing? With some hesitation we will admit that they were. Presumably the possessors of Messrs. Dent's pretty edition, or of any edition for that matter, will be glad to set this small volume beside the others and thus become owners of the complete prose works of an English classic. For Peacock is a classic; otherwise they might well have been allowed to acquire that portentous dignity which grows like moss on ancient and unprinted MSS. in the British Museum. Here and there, in the farces, one may discover examples of truly "Peacockian" wit and style, but these rare gems have mostly been worked into the novels; while the residue, which includes a drama in blank verse, has little if any intrinsic value. The earliest works of Peacock—a brilliant amateur to the last—are as amateurish as the earliest works of his friend Shelley and as thin and conventional as the worst of Goldoni. Nevertheless they are readable; so we need not stay to quarrel with the enthusiastic editor who claims that they are "replete with fun, written in a flexible style, and bearing the imprint of a scholarly discrimination."

English prose and humour are certainly the richer for one or two speeches in this little book, but the service it performs, or can be made to perform, is greater than that of rescuing a few fragments of humorous prose or even of filling a gap on our shelves. It sends us back to perhaps the least known of the great English, writers. The "Life" of Peacock has yet to be written: an ineffectual memoir by Sir Henry Cole, some personal recollections by the author's granddaughter Mrs. Clarke, a critical essay from the versatile but vapid pen of Lord Houghton, the gossip of Robert Buchanan, and editorial notices by Prof. Saintsbury and the late Richard Garnett, together afford nothing more than a perfunctory appreciation. Two writers, indeed, have attempted a more elaborate estimate: James Spedding, an able prig,[5] reviewed Peacock's novels in the *Edinburgh* of January 1839, and more than half a century later Mr. Herbert Paul contributed to the *Nineteenth Century* a paper on the same subject. Unluckily, the judgment of both is vitiated by a common defect. Both are good journalists, but both are better party men; consequently, neither can appreciate the attitude of one to whom collective wisdom was folly, who judged every question in politics, philosophy, literature, and art on its merits, and whose scorn for those who judged otherwise was expressed without any of those obliging circumlocutions that are prized so highly in political life. With the possible exception of Prof. Saintsbury, not one of Peacock's interpreters has understood his position or shared his point of view; did not Dr. Arthur Button Young, the editor of these plays, himself affirm that

> "his stories deal with tangible realities, and not with obscure or absurd situations, as is the case with those of many novelists.... For this reason alone they deserve to be widely known, as also their author, for having helped to raise the tone of novel-writing at a critical juncture in its development, by introducing into his tales instruction and information"?

> It is only fair to add that this bit of criticism occurs in his "Inaugural Dissertation presented to the Philosophical Faculty of the University of Freiburg im Breisgau for the Asquisition of the Degree of Doctor of Philosophy."

In calling Peacock a great writer we have raised a claim that needs some support. His exquisite style with its Tacitean flavour, the perfection of his lyrics, his wit, and that intellectual brilliancy which sparkles from all the facets of his satire, parody, and epigram, suffice to endear him to the small, fastidious world whose approval is best worth having, and also, perhaps, to justify our opinion. But, unless we mistake, the appeal of his novels goes farther than the frontiers of good taste. Peacock's mind was original; he thought about many things and he did his own thinking. He is the other side to every question; his way of looking at life is a perpetual challenge; and a man without a vestige of humour or taste may read him with profit for his point of view.

Peacock belongs to no school or age. He has been called a man of the eighteenth century living in the nineteenth; nothing could be farther from the truth. He loved the sense and dignity of the Augustans, just as he loved the fire and romance of the Renaissance, and the mysterious gaiety of the Middle Ages; but he could have criticized any of them with as good a will as he criticized the age of machinery and "the march of mind," and, had he been born in any one of them, would doubtless have done so. He was a student of bardic poetry who yet admired Ariosto; his passion for classical literature was uncommonly wise and sincere; he read Sophocles for pleasure. So remote was he from the eighteenth-century Grecians that he could perceive and enjoy the romantic element in Greek life and art; yet it is a mistake to call him a Greek. An Athenian of the time of Pericles was, he thought, the noblest specimen of humanity that history had to show, and of that nobility he assimilated what he could. He acquired a distaste for cant, prudery, facile emotion, and philanthropy; he learnt to enjoy the good things of life without fear or shame; to love strength and beauty, and to respect the truth. For all that, he was a modern too; sharp eyes can see it in his verse. A touch of gloating and uninquisitive wonder, a suspicion of sentiment for sentiment's sake, the ghost of an appeal from the head to the heart, from the certainty of the present to the mystery of the past and the future, betray the descendant of Shakespeare and Sterne. The very culture that he inherited from a Græco-Roman civilization, his bookishness, his archæology, his conscious Paganism, would have looked queer in an Athenian of the fifth century B.C. The author of "Love and Age" was no Greek; but he was Greek enough to stand out above his fellows, from whom he is most honourably distinguished by his Athenian open-mindedness.

That Peacock cultivated prejudices is not disputed; for instance, he could not abide tobacco-smoke, Lord Brougham, or the Great Exhibition of 1851. But his prejudices were as peculiar to himself as were the principles of Sir Thomas Browne. They were not the prejudices of his age and state, neither were they of the kind that is fatal to free thinking and plain speaking. Unlike the popular dogmas of the muscular Christians and their rivals the muscular agnostics, his whims and fancies were superficial and involved no intellectual confusion. He compelled no one to build on unproved hypotheses, nor would he suffer himself to be compelled. Though sceptical about progress and mistrustful of democracy, to the end of his life he disliked the Conservative party; and perhaps his finest flights of sarcasm occur in "The Misfortunes of Elphin," where he ridicules Canning's florid rhetoric in defence of the Constitution.

> "'Reports have been brought to me [says Elphin], that the embankment, which has been so long entrusted to your care, is in a state of dangerous decay.'
>
> "'Decay,' said Seithenyn, 'is one thing, and danger is another. Everything that is old must decay. That the embankment is old, I am free to confess; that it is somewhat rotten in parts, I will not altogether deny; that it is any the worse for that, I do most sturdily gainsay. It does its business well: it works well: it keeps out the water from the land, and it lets in the wine upon the High Commission of Embankment. Cupbearer, fill. Our ancestors were wiser than we: they built it in their wisdom; and, if we should be so rash as to try to mend it, we should only mar it.'

"'The stonework,' said Teithrin, 'is sapped and mined: the piles are rotten, broken, and dislocated: the floodgates and sluices are leaky and creaky.'

"'That is the beauty of it,' said Seithenyn. 'Some parts of it are rotten, and some parts of it are sound.'

"'It is well,' said Elphin, 'that some parts are sound: it were better that all were so.'

"'So I have heard some people say before,' said Seithenyn; 'perverse people, blind to venerable antiquity: that very unamiable sort of people, who are in the habit of indulging their reason. But I say, the parts that are rotten give elasticity to those that are sound: they give them elasticity, elasticity, elasticity. If it were all sound, it would break by its own obstinate stiffness: the soundness is checked by the rottenness, and the stiffness is balanced by the elasticity. There is nothing so dangerous as innovation. See the waves in the equinoctial storms, dashing and clashing, roaring and pouring, spattering and battering, rattling and battling against it. I would not be so presumptious as to say, I could build anything that would stand against them half an hour; and here this immortal old work, which God forbid the finger of modern mason should bring into jeopardy, this immortal work has stood for centuries, and will stand for centuries more, if we let it alone. It is well: it works well: let well alone. Cupbearer, fill. It was half rotten when I was born, and that is a conclusive reason why it should be three parts rotten when I die.'"

Peacock's attitude towards women affords an example of the liberality of his views and of his isolation. It shocked Victorian sentimentalists, and would probably infuriate the more austere feminists of to-day. His heroines, like all his characters, are roughly and extravagantly sketched; what makes them peculiar is that they are sometimes almost alive. Stupidity, ignorance, and incompetence, craven submissiveness or insipid resignation, he did not commend in women: on the contrary, intellect, wit, gaiety, spirit, and even a first in the Classical Tripos seemed or would have seemed desirable and ladylike attributes to the creator of Anthelia Melincourt and Morgana Gryll. What was called "womanliness" in the forties displeased him; but he liked women to be feminine, and knew that distinguished women have ever been distinguished as women.

The truth is, Peacock had standards tested by which the current ideas of almost any age would be found wanting. Without being a profound thinker, he was one of those people who "bother about ends" to the extent of being unwilling to approve of means unless they are satisfied that the end in view is good—or at least that there is some end in view. With a self-complacent age, in which every one was shouting "Forward!" and no one was expected to inquire "Whither?" he was necessarily out of sympathy. To the shouters he seemed irrational and irrelevant. They called him "immoral" when they were solemn, and "whimsical" when they were merry; and "whimsical" is the epithet with which we are tempted to label him, if labelled he must be. Genius makes strange bedfellows; and Peacock's intellectual candour finds itself associated with the emotional capriciousness of Sterne. Truly, he is always unexpected, and as often as not superficially inconsequent. To state the three parts of a syllogism is not in his way; and by implication he challenged half the major premises in vogue. His scorn of rough-and-ready standards, commonplaces, and what used to be called "the opinion of all sensible men" made him disrespectful to common sense. It was common sense once to believe that the sun went round the earth, and it is still the mark of a sensible man to ignore, on occasions, the law of contradictions. To that common sense which is compounded of mental sluggishness and a taste for being in the majority Peacock's wit was a needle. He was intellectual enough to enjoy pricking bladders, and so finished a performer that we never tire of watching him at his play.

He was, in fact, an artist with intellectual curiosity; and just as he lacked the depth of a philosopher so he wanted the vision of a poet. That he possessed genius will not be denied; but his art is fanciful rather than imaginative and of creative power he had next to none. His life was neither a mission nor a miracle. But he was blessed with that keen delight in his own sensations which makes a world full of beautiful and amusing things, charming people, wine, and warm sunshine seem, on the whole, a very tolerable place, and all metaphysical speculation and political passion a little unnecessary. He made an art of living, and his novels are a part of his life. He wrote them because he had a subtle sense of the ludicrous, a turn for satire, and style. He wrote because he enjoyed writing; and, with a disregard for the public inconceivable in a man of sense, he wrote the sort of books that he himself would have liked to read. They are the sort, we think, that will always be worth reading.

Athenæum Oct. 1911

> "Between the publication of his [Peacock's] first and last poem sixty years had elapsed; but the records of his existence would, if placed in close juxtaposition, hardly fill out ten years."

Thus writes Mr. Freeman; and Mr. Van Doren's book is a failure just because he has insisted on expanding those records into a volume of three hundred pages. Of such a work a great part must consist in stating trivial facts and drawing from them inferences which there is no reason to accept, and which would be unimportant if accepted.

> "About the time of the publication of 'Palmyra,' the young poet went back to Chertsey to live. His grandfather, Thomas Love, died December 10, 1805, and Mrs. Love, thus left alone, probably desired the companionship of her daughter and grandson. A letter to Hookham, dated two years later, testifies that Peacock soon extended one of his walking tours much farther than he had hitherto gone, in an excursion to Scotland."

Here follows an extract from a rather gushing and quite unimportant letter about the beauties of Scotch scenery, after which the paragraph concludes as follows:

> "Nothing further is known of this Scottish tour, but from it probably dates Peacock's inveterate prejudice against the Scotch."

This is Mr. Van Doren at his worst and hack biography at normal. At his best he gives a straightforward account of the little that industry can unearth concerning a writer of first-rate importance who died but fifty-five years ago and whose life is yet more obscure than that of many a smaller man who has been dead twice or thrice as long. Industry in quest of facts is, indeed, Mr. Van Doren's chief merit, which only aggravates our surprise and regret at his having concluded his researches without discovering that Old Sarum is not in Cornwall. Still, he has written a readable book. His knowledge of English is superior to that of the majority of his compatriots; and when he is not trying to be caustic or facetious he is often quite sensible. We can say no more for him however.

Mr. Freeman aims higher, and though he comes short of his mark his is a valuable book. He can write well, and will write better; at present he is set upon being witty and clever, which is the more to be regretted in that he is both by nature. He has a view of life and letters which, if it be literary and rather superficial, is, at all events, personal. Perceiving the insufficiency of material for a biography, he has attempted an appreciation of Peacock's art. As we set ourselves a similar task so recently as February last, when reviewing Dr. Young's edition of the plays, we feel no call to restate our estimate or pit it against that of this new critic. It need only be said that he realizes, as does Mr. Van Doren, the singularity of Peacock's genius; that, though neither has succeeded in showing precisely why it is unique, the English critic has brought forward some highly illuminating suggestions; and that reduction by a half would be the greatest improvement that either book could undergo.

In the circumstances, our interest tends to centre on the biographical parts of both works. For both are biographical: only Mr. Freeman, who claims attention for judgment rather than for learning, has been at less pains to sift and record the minute evidence that contemporary literature and journalism afford. Fresh evidence, in the shape of letters and memoirs, may, of course, be brought forward; until then these two volumes will be final. So far as external evidence goes, the student is now in possession of all that is known about the author of "Headlong Hall."

It is surprising that Mr. Freeman's tact did not rescue him from the temptation into which Mr. Van Doren's industry led him inevitably—the temptation of finding in Peacock's mature work definable traces of childish memories and impressions. Still more surprising is it that, when both have quoted much that is worthless, neither should have printed the one significant document amongst the surviving fragments of his boyhood. This is a letter in verse to his mother, which not only gives promise of the songs that, above all else, have made their author famous, but is also worth quoting for its peculiar charm and fancy. Unless we mistake, it has only once been printed, and is hardly known to the literary public, so here it is:

Dear Mother,

I attempt to write you a letter

In verse, tho' in prose I could do it much better;

The Muse, this cold weather, sleeps up at Parnassus,

And leaves us poor poets as stupid as asses.

She'll tarry still longer, if she has a warm chamber,

A store of old massie, ambrosia, and amber.

Dear mother, don't laugh, you may think she is tipsy
And I, if a poet, must drink like a gipsy.

    Suppose I should borrow the horse of Jack Stenton—
A finer ridden beast no muse ever went on—
Pegasus' fleet wings perhaps now are frozen,
I'll send her old Stenton's, I know I've well chosen;
Be it frost, be it thaw, the horse can well canter;
The sight of the beast cannot help to enchant her.

    All the boys at our school are well, tho' yet many
Are suffered, at home, to suck eggs with their granny.

    "To-morrow," says daddy, "you must go, my dear Billy,
To Englefield House; do not cry, you are silly."
Says the mother, all dressed in silk and in satin,
"Don't cram the poor boy with your Greek and your Latin,
I'll have him a little longer before mine own eyes,
To nurse him and feed him with tarts and mince-pies;
We'll send him to school when the weather is warmer;
Come kiss me, my pretty, my sweet little charmer!"

    But now I must banish all fun and all folly,
So doleful's the news I am going to tell ye:
Poor Wade, my schoolfellow, lies low in the gravel,
One month ere fifteen put an end to his travel;
Harmless and mild, and remark'd for good nature;
The cause of his death was his overgrown stature:
His epitaph I wrote, as inserted below;
What tribute more friendly could I on him bestow?

    The bard craves one shilling of his own dear mother,
And, if you think proper, add to it another.

That epitaph is better known, but deserves to be better still:

Here lies interred, in silent shade,

The frail remains of Hamlet Wade;

A youth more promising ne'er took breath;

But ere fifteen laid cold in death!

Ye young, ye old, and ye of middle age,

Act well your part, for quit the stage

Of mortal life, one day you must,

And, like him, crumble into dust.

Surely the boy of nine years old who wrote this was destined to be something better than a minor poet. And did not the delightful mother who encouraged him to express himself deserve something better for her son? Indeed, he must have been an enchanting child, with his long, flaxen curls, bright colouring, and fine, intelligent head. One fancies him a happy creature, making light work of his Greek and Latin grammar at Mr. Wicks's school on Englefield Green, at home spoilt and educated, in the best and most literal sense of the word, by his pretty mother and his gallant old grandfather. No wonder Queen Charlotte, driving in Windsor Park, stopped her carriage and got down to kiss the winsome little boy.

From Peacock's youth and early writings (he was born in 1785 and published "Palmyra" in 1806) we can gather some idea of his character. The obvious thing about him is his cleverness. The question is, What will he make of it? He tries business for a short time; the sea for an even shorter; and then he settles down in the country to a life of study and composition: he will be a man of letters. His poems are what we should expect a clever lad to write. Had they been written at the end of the nineteenth century doubtless they would have been as fashionably decadent as, written at the beginning, they are fashionably pompous. It was clear from the first that Peacock would not be a poet; he lacked the essential quality—the power of feeling deeply. Before he was twenty it must have been clear that he possessed a remarkable head and an ordinary heart. He had wits enough for anything and sufficient feeling and imagination to write a good song; but in these early days his intellect served chiefly to save him from sentimentality and the grosser kinds of rhetoric. It gained him a friend too, and that friend was Shelley.

To think of Peacock's youth is to think of his relations with Shelley. He seems to have given more than he received: his nature was not receptive. He made the poet read Greek, and persuaded him that he was not infected with elephantiasis by quoting Lucretius "to the effect that the disease was known to exist on the banks of the Nile, *neque præterea usquam*." These words were "the greatest comfort to Shelley." The two young men did a vast amount of walking, arguing, and miscellaneous reading together, in which Peacock, partly from conviction and partly from affectation, seems to have been pretty consistent in performing the office of a wet blanket. Testing his intellect on other people's enthusiasms, falling sedately and whimsically in love with various ladies, amongst them his future wife, but keeping such feelings as he had for the most part to himself, Peacock slipped through all the critical stages of youth till in 1816 he published "Headlong Hall." Brains will not make a poet, but they made a superb satirist.

There is nothing to puzzle us in Peacock's accepting a post under the East India Company. An unusually strong inclination toward Miss Jane Gryffydh, his "milk-white Snowdonian Antelope" as Shelley calls her, whom he had not seen for more than eight years, and to whom he became engaged without further inspection, may possibly have counted for something in his decision. But the obvious explanation is that a man who lives by the head needs regular employment, and only he who lives by the emotions has anything to lose by it. Peacock's feelings were not so fine that routine could blunt them, nor so deep that an expression of them could give a satisfactory purpose to life. He entered the Company's service at the age of four-and-thirty; he found in it congenial friends, congenial employment, and a salary that enabled him to indulge his rather luxurious tastes. He kept chambers in London, a house on the Thames, a good cellar we may be sure, and a wife. Of this part of his life we know little beyond the fact that he was an able and industrious official. Probably, we shall not be far wrong in supposing him to have been much like other officials, only more intelligent, more witty, more sceptical, more learned, and more "cranky": also he kept stored somewhere at the back of his mind a spark of that mysterious thing called genius. At any rate, his recorded opinion, "There has never been anything perfect under the sun except the compositions of Mozart," smacks strongly of classical concerts and the Treasury.

Though during this period he wrote his most entertaining, and perhaps his most brilliant novel, "Crotchet Castle," the years were heavy with misfortune. His mother, the human being for whom he seems to have cared most, died in 1833; before that date his wife had become a hopeless invalid. Three of his four children were dead before he retired from affairs. Already he had outlived many of his companions. Sorrow does not seem to have embittered but neither did it sweeten greatly his temper. His reticence stiffened, so did his prejudices. Only emotion enables a man to make something noble and lovely of pain; but intellect teaches him to bear it like a gentleman.

It is easy to draw a pleasant picture of Peacock's old age; deeply considered, however, it is profoundly sad. He had stood for many great causes but for none had he stood greatly. Good nature and benevolence had done duty for love and pity. He had been more intimate with books than with men. And so, at the end, he found himself alone. His tragedy is not that he was lonely, but that he preferred to be so. He retired with a handsome pension to a sheltered life at Halliford. The jolly old pagan, the scholar, and the caustic satirist were still alive in him. He wrote "Gryll Grange." He packed poor Robert Buchanan out of the house for smoking in it. He terrified a meek curate, who came to persuade him to leave his burning home, by shouting at him, "By the immortal gods I will not move." He carried on a desultory correspondence with Lord Broughton, full of literary humour and literary sentiment. He practised small benevolences and small tyrannies, liked to see smiling faces about him, and declined to believe seriously in the unhappiness of others. He was a thoroughly good-natured, selfish old man.

In old age he had to pay the penalty that awaits those who live by the head and not by the heart. He had kind acquaintances, but he had no real friends. He had nothing to look back upon but a series of more or less amusing events and a tale of successful achievements—no high enterprises, no splendid failures, no passionate affections. Before him lay nothing but his books, his dinner, and a literary reputation. Capable biographers can make pretty pictures of the white-haired scholar surrounded by his favourite authors. They can turn his petulant limitations and querulous prejudices into exquisite foibles, his despotisms into quaint impetuosity, his insensibility to human want and misery into mellow wisdom. But we cannot forget that the last years of those who have never passionately pursued impossible ideals or loved imperfect human beings are probably more attractive to the biographers who record than to the men and women who have to endure them.

FOOTNOTES:

[4] "The Plays of Thomas Love Peacock." Published for the first time. Edited by A. B. Young. (David Nutt.)

[5] The week after this article appeared Sir Frederick Pollock wrote to the *Athenæum* complaining of my having called Spedding a prig. Well, here is a sample of what Spedding has to say about "Melincourt":

> "Had the business ended here we should have thought
> that the author's better genius had prevailed. We might

indeed have questioned many of his doctrines, both social and political; and shown cause to doubt whether in the faithful bosom of real nature they would yield so fair a harvest as in the more accommodating soil of fiction. But we should have met him with undivided sympathy, as no idle talker on no idle theme. This, however, his worst genius interferes to prevent. He has only a half faith in the cause he has espoused, and dares not let go his interest with the other party. It is as if, having, in sport or curiosity, raised the veil of truth, he had felt rebuked by the severity of her aspect, and turned for relief to more than usual levity and mockery. Hence the perpetual interruption of the serious and affecting, and sometimes even awful, interest which belongs to the main argument of the piece, by scenes of farcical and extravagant caricature which might be pleasant enough as varieties in that farce of unreason with which he usually entertains us, but which, coming upon the mind in a state of serious emotion, are offensive and disagreeable. The two styles appear two opposite and incompatible moods; and it is impossible so to govern the imagination or the sympathies as to be in the humour for both. If you are not disgusted with the lighter, you cannot but be wearied with the graver."

And again:

"As it is, this affected contrast [the contrast which Spedding thinks Peacock may have intended between the beauty of Forester and Anthelia's view of life, and the "gross pictures of corruption, quackery, and worldliness" with which he surrounds them], instead of bringing the virtue of his hero into stronger relief, serves only to make more conspicuous his own want of constancy in his purpose and faith in his principles."

Spedding solemnly proceeds to give Peacock a little advice about the construction of his novels, and recommends that "Melincourt" should be divided into two stories: one to deal with the adventures of Sir Oran Haut-ton and his election for the borough of Onevote; the other to treat of "the graver questions concerning the realizations of the spirit of chivalry under the forms of modern society ... with Forester and Anthelia for the central figures."

"If he would but set about this latter task in a faithful spirit, we do not fear to predict, from the specimen which the tale before us, even in its present state, exhibits, that he would produce a work of far higher and more enduring interest than any he has yet attempted."

Let the reader consider "Melincourt," what manner of work it is, and then judge faithfully between me and Sir Fred.

[6] "The Life of Thomas Love Peacock," By Carl Van Doren. (Dent and Sons.)

"Thomas Love Peacock." By A. Martin Freeman. (Martin Secker.)

———————————

BOSWELL'S LETTERS[7]

Athenæum Feb. 1909

Boswell's letters enjoy the advantage of a mysterious history. They were written between 1758 and 1795, not without a view to publication, but were lost for more than fifty years. At Boulogne in 1850 Major Stone, of the East India Company, had the fortunate curiosity to examine a scrap of paper in which was wrapped some small purchase; it turned out to be a letter signed by James Boswell, and was traced to the store of an itinerant paper-vendor, where the letters published in 1856 were discovered. The anonymous editor of this issue is conjectured—with good reason, as we think—by Mr. Seccombe, who introduces the volume, to have been a Philip Francis of the Middle Temple who became later Sir Philip of the Supreme Consular Court of the Levant; but this matter also is obscure. The strangest mystery of all, however, is that these interesting, entertaining, in fact delightful letters, though on their first appearance they created a mild literary sensation, till last December had never been reprinted.

The volume before us is a reprint from the first edition, the introduction by Mr. Seccombe being substituted for that of the original editor. We wish that Mr. Seccombe had been less modest—less conservative at any rate. With his view that "the editing was admirably done" we cannot agree entirely. Francis, who has intercalated blocks of exegesis and comment between the letters, writes good, straightforward prose, and appears to have been a good, sensible sort of man. He has enlivened his editorial labours with irruptions of legal facetiousness and sagacious reflections. He admires Carlyle. But his lack of subtlety and his prodigious good sense make him incapable of appreciating the character of Boswell. Passages in the letters which seemed to him ridiculous he, in his solicitude for the reader's enjoyment, has been careful to print in italics; for it is difficult to suppose that Boswell underlined them himself. The originals are again lost; should the passages in question really be underlined, it would follow that Boswell was not unintentionally or unconsciously ridiculous; that all his life he practised an elaborate mystification; that he succeeded in hoodwinking the world; that he enlightened Temple alone, who nevertheless appears to have treated him as though he were what the world took him for; and that Francis, who saw these underlined manuscripts, and yet persisted in the conventional view of Boswell, was not a Mid-Victorian prig but a common imbecile. It is true that he has been stupid enough to mangle and emasculate the letters that he was employed to publish; an officious prude unquestionably he was, but no fool, much less an idiot.

To discuss the character of Boswell has ever been a delicate, not to say dangerous, undertaking; but at least we may affirm that those who, judging him from the "Life of Johnson," are dissatisfied with the ordinary, unfavourable view, will not be put out of countenance by these letters. To be sure they will not be disappointed of the popular "Bozzy," ridiculous, vain, and a little vulgar, something of a snob, of a sycophant even, with an undignified zeal for notoriety and an imperfect moral sense; but beside him they will find another Boswell, the friend of Hume and Johnson, with his passion for excellence, generous nature, good understanding, and genius for observation—a man by no means to be despised. They will see how this man expresses thoughts and feelings, often sufficiently commonplace, in words so astonishingly appropriate that we are amazed by the sheer truth of the self-revelation; and they may even conjecture that some of his performances, which have been lightly attributed to dull self-complacency or a defective sense of proportion, are more probably the effects of a whimsical and fantastic mind through which ran possibly a queer strain of madness. Be that as it may, we now select for quotation a few characteristic passages, leaving the reader to decide for himself when and how far Boswell is laughing at "Bozzy."

The correspondence with Temple, a fellow-student at Edinburgh, began in 1758, when Boswell was eighteen; for the first eight years, however, he was too busy making acquaintance with Johnson, travelling on the Continent, and conducting his famous Corsican adventure, to be a very prolific letter-writer. In 1766 he settled down in Edinburgh to the law, which he found intolerably dreary, and a love-affair, which he found too exciting. "The dear infidel," as he called her, besides being another man's wife, seems to have been an extravagant and disreputable young woman:

> "In a former part of this letter I have talked a great deal of my sweet little mistress; I am, however, uneasy about her. Furnishing a house and maintaining her with a maid will cost me a great deal of money, and it is too like marriage, or too much a settled plan of licentiousness; but what can I do?

> "Besides, she is ill-bred, quite a rompish girl. She debases my dignity; she has no refinement, but she is very handsome and very lively."

What he did was to break with her; four weeks later he writes:

"My life is one of the most romantic that I believe either you or I really know of; and yet I am a very sensible, good sort of man. What is the meaning of this, Temple? You may depend upon it that very soon my follies will be at an end, and I shall turn out an admirable member of society. Now that I have given my mind the turn, I am totally emancipated from my charmer, as much as from the gardener's daughter who now puts on my fire and performs menial offices like any other wench; and yet just this time twelve month I was so madly in love as to think of marrying her."

The frequency and solemnity of Boswell's resolutions to amend are extraordinary, though the fact that his correspondent was a curate suggests an explanation; in carrying them out he was perfectly normal.

Boswell tells us that he "looks with horror on adultery," and the love-affairs with which his letters overflow appear, for the most part, to have been sufficiently innocent; for an "Italian angel," Zelide (whom he knew at Utrecht), Miss Bosville, and "La Belle Irlandaise" he cherished at different times a chaste flame; while Miss Blair, a neighbour and lady of fortune, very nearly caught him. But Boswell decided that he would not have a "Scots lass." "You cannot say how fine a woman I may marry; perhaps a Howard or some other of the noblest in the kingdom." "Rouse me, my friend!" he cries; "Kate has not fire enough; she does not know the value of her lover!" Nevertheless, he was to have a "Scots lass" after all, for in the autumn of 1769 he married Miss Margaret Montgomerie, "a true Montgomerie, whom I esteem, whom I love, after fifteen years, as on the day when she gave me her hand" ("Letter to the People of Scotland").

After his marriage Boswell's life continued agitated and desultory: he practised at the Scotch Bar, without much success, and was called to the English; almost every year he visited London, where he cultivated Johnson, enjoyed good company and fine, made the most of his social and literary importance, and revelled in the genuine and flattering friendship of Paoli, who seems to have made him free of his house: "I felt more dignity when I had several servants at my devotion, a large apartment, and the convenience and state of a coach."

It was absurd of him, no doubt, to say, "Am I not fortunate in having something about me that interests most people at first sight in my favour?" but it seems to have been near the truth. "I am really the great man now. I have had David Hume in the forenoon, and Mr. Johnson in the afternoon."

These great men were interested somehow, and so, one must suppose, was Miss Silverton:

> "There is a Miss Silverton in the Fly with me, an amiable creature, who has been in France. I can unite little fondnesses with perfect conjugal love."

There was, too, "an agreeable young widow" who, also in a fly, "nursed me, and supported my lame foot on her knee."

Boswell's life in Edinburgh was not happy; he hated the rough society of Scotch lawyers, and quarrelled with his father, the Laird of Auchinleck, who seems to have been a tiresome, disagreeable old man. The Laird died in 1782, and seven years later Boswell lost his "valuable wife." His story becomes melancholy: money troubles and family perplexities beset him (he was left with five children); and it may be that what once made him odd, aggravated by his breaking health, now made him gloomy. After his wife's death he came to London for good. Already he had taken a house in Queen Anne Street, and here he worked hard at "The Life," comforted a little by his assurance that it would be a masterpiece:

> "I am absolutely certain that my mode of biography, which gives not only a *History* of Johnson's *visible* progress through the world, and of his publications, but a *view* of his mind in his letters and conversations, is the most perfect that can be conceived, and will be more of a Life than any work that has ever yet appeared."

With this bold but just prophecy we may leave him; he died in 1795.

FOOTNOTE:

[7] "Letters of James Boswell to the Rev. W. J. Temple." (Sidgwick and Jackson.)

CARLYLE'S LOVES AND LOVE-LETTERS[8]

I

Athenæum May and Oct. 1909

Are people still interested in the Carlyles? Some are, we suppose. The older generation is interested in Carlyle, at any rate; though the younger, we believe, is not. For men and women under thirty the redoubtable sage has apparently no message; but for many of their fathers and mothers his least word still has a certain importance.

Such reverent curiosity, though it may excuse some bad books and much futile research, will, we fear, hardly justify the volume before us—Mr. Archibald's we mean, which tells us little about Carlyle and that little by no means new. One chapter only can be manufactured out of his sufficiently indefinite relations with Miss Gordon; though ten more pages are filled out with a discussion of that wholly unimportant question "Who was Blumine?" The reasonable conjecture is, of course, that Carlyle's method resembled that of other writers; his heroine, no doubt, was the child of his own imagination, and when a model was needed he drew indiscriminately from the ladies with whom he was acquainted.

Should any one chance to be interested in Margaret Gordon, her ancestors, her kindred, or her husband, he may glean a certain amount of information from this book. Born at Charlottetown (Prince Edward Island) in 1798, she was left fatherless at the age of four, and brought up in Scotland by her aunt. Between 1818 and 1820 she may have had a love-affair or flirtation with Carlyle; and in 1824 she married Mr. Bannerman, a commonplace, good-humoured business-man from Aberdeen, who became a Member of Parliament. Mr. Bannerman speculated, lost his fortune, and was consoled with a colonial governorship and a knighthood. Lady Bannerman was drawn into the Evangelical movement, devoted the last years of her life to works of piety, and died (1878) in a little house at Greenwich and the odour of sanctity. As to what manner of woman she may have been we are left in ignorance; into her mode of thinking, feeling, and seeing—into her character, that is—Mr. Archibald has obtained no insight. The necessary changes in matters of history having been made, his volume might do duty as the biographical memoir of thousands of her contemporaries. But perhaps a couple of specimens of the style and substance of Mr. Archibald's prose will best give the measure of his understanding:

"Lady Bannerman dispensed the hospitality of Government House with the dignity and grace which might be expected of one who for over thirty years had moved in the best society of England. She had the power of putting all at their ease, of identifying herself with their individual interests, and of entering with animation into the affairs of the hour. But while she was kind and gracious and frank, and would freely enter into conversation with any one, there was always a certain dignity which prevented any attempt at undue familiarity."

Again:

"In St. John's she was exceedingly kind and charitable to the poor, and she and Lady Hoyles were active workers in the Dorcas Society. She worshipped at St. Thomas' (Episcopal) Church, and was especially interested in her Sunday-school class. As we have seen, her sympathies were more with the Presbyterian Church, but probably because of her husband's official position, she always chose in the Colonies to connect herself with the Church of England."

If this be a fair account of Lady Bannerman, we may be pardoned for wondering why any one thought her biography worth writing. What it all has to do with Carlyle is to us far from clear. The eyes of publishers, however, are in these matters notoriously sharper than those of reviewers.

II

Having disposed of Carlyle's first love, we can attend to his second—if that is where Miss Welsh comes in order of seniority; for our text mercifully obliges us to say nothing of Miss Aurora Kirkpatrick, another claimant to the honour of having sat for Blumine, while on the glories of Lady Ashburton, who, to be frank, interests us no more than the simplest of these extremely simple "misses," the title of our essay precludes us from expatiating. But can we? Does not the great man, who was to give Jane the splendour of his name, seem rather to demand prompt satisfaction for the insult paid him in our first paragraph? There we said, or implied, that he was obsolescent; and it is, perhaps, worth pausing to inquire how a man who seemed to his own age one of the great teachers and spiritual masters of humanity—the peer of Pythagoras and Buddha, of Plato, Epictetus, St. Francis and Rousseau—comes in this generation to be held a little higher than Emerson, a good deal lower than Matthew Arnold, immeasurably so than Renan. And is it not worth pausing again to reflect that, contemporaneously with these men, and almost unknown to Western

Europe, lived one who bids fair to produce a greater effect on the world than has been produced by any teacher since the crucifixion?

It was primarily as a teacher, as a disseminator of ideas, that Carlyle appeared venerable to his own age; in a less degree they admired him as an historian and an artist. To-day, his ideas are as musty as those of Godwin— a better exponent of deeper speculations: as an historian—in spite of an undeniable gift for visualizing and describing scenes from the past—he is hardly of more consequence than Creighton or Stanhope: while, as an artist, he ranks with such faded rhetoricians as Châteaubriand.

What is the meaning of this? Why simply that the Victorians made the mistake about Carlyle that every age makes about its Carlyles. They took a thoughtful journalist for a master; and this they did because the journalist had the skill and conviction to persuade them, and himself, that what is commonest and most vigorous in human nature is also most sublime. Carlyle could, in perfect good faith, give tone to the vulgar instincts and passions; he could make narrow-mindedness, brutality, intolerance, obtuseness, and sentimentality seem noble; he knew, being an unconscious hypocrite, how, without a glimmer of open cynicism, to make the best of both worlds. For instance, Carlyle and his public wished to believe in Eternal Justice regulating the affairs of men. They believed in it as something emotionally congenial to them, not, you may be sure, as a metaphysical truth discovered and confirmed by the intellect. Intellectual processes were not in Carlyle's way: he was a popular philosopher. From this belief in Eternal Justice he naturally deduced the doctrine that Right is Might, which doctrine applied to history bore fruit most grateful to hero-worshippers—a sect that flourished uncommonly in those days. When, however, it was pointed out by earthy and eristic rationalists that if in the past Right was Might then it followed that Might was Right, Carlyle, who had ever the shortest of ways with dissenters, drowned the argument in a flood of invective. Of course if Right is Might it does follow that the good cause has always been the successful one; and in that case it looks as though the successful one must always have been the good. Might, in fact, is Right. Carlyle knew better: and he who would be the prophet of his age must know, as he did, to reject unwholesome conclusions without invalidating the healthy premises from which they follow.

Each age has its Carlyles, but it never much respects the Carlyles of other ages. We have our Ferrero and our H. G. Wells, to say nothing of such small fry as Faguets, Marinetti, *e tutti quanti.* They are people who have something for their own age and nothing for any other, and their own age is pretty sure to prefer them to any great man it may produce but fail to smother: they are adored and duly forgotten. They must come forward as the critics and guides of society; whether they declare their messages in prose or verse, in novels, histories, speeches, essays, or philosophical treatises is of no consequence. It must be possible to make prophets of them, that is all. A pure artist or philosopher or man of science, one who is concerned with Beauty or Truth but not with its application to contemporary life will not do. Darwin and Swinburne, therefore, the greatest of the English Victorians, were not eligible; but the age chose Carlyle for its select preacher when it might have had Mill. Naturally it preferred his coloured rhetoric and warm sentimentality to Mill's cold reason and white-hot emotion. It chose him because he was what Mill was not—a Carlyle. Yet, though Utilitarianism is discredited, Mill remains; the candour and subtlety of his intellect impress us still, and his Autobiography will seem to future generations one of the most moving documents of the nineteenth century.

As for Carlyle, "nobody marks him"; we only wonder that he will still be talking. The old controversy between those who wish to believe the truth and those who insist that what they wish to believe is true raves on; but neither side dreams of briefing the Chelsea sage. His vatic eloquence carries no conviction. Men and women of the younger generation, whatever their views, find no support in him, because he appeals to axioms and postulates which to them seem unreal. It is not that his arguments are old-fashioned, but that they are based on nothing and apply to nothing. A modern emotionalist may call in Tolstoy or Bergson or Berkley or Léon Bloy or Péguy or Plato himself to break the head of Anatole France or Bertrand Russell, but he will not trouble Carlyle. And besides finding him empty, the new age is quite aware of his positive defects. It cannot away with his peasant morality—moralizing rather—his provincialism, and the grossness of his method. From the beginning to the end of his works there is neither pure thought nor pure feeling—nothing but a point of view which is now perceived to be ridiculously plebeian. Nevertheless, Carlyle had one positive gift that the younger generation is perhaps not very well qualified to appreciate, he was an extraordinarily capable man of letters. His footnotes, for instance, might serve as models; he had a prodigious talent for picking out just those bits of by-information that will amuse and interest a reader and send him back to the text with renewed attention. His editing of Mrs. Carlyle's letters—letters which come not within our terms of reference and from which, therefore, we cannot decently quote—is remarkable: only, even here, his intolerable virtue and vanity, his callous self-content, his miserable, misplaced self-pity and his nauseous sentimentality parade themselves on almost every page. For all his "Oh heavenses," "courageous little souls," and "ay de mis," he never once guessed the nature of his offence, never realized the beastliness of that moral and religious humbug which to himself seems always to have justified him in playing tyrant and vampire to a woman of genius.

III

The volumes before us, as we have hinted, were expected, not without excitement, by those people for whose benefit we are about to review them. It must be confessed that they have not wholly escaped the fate that is apt to befall the progeny of parturient mountains. Not that they are precisely what Horace would have expected them to be: they are anything but small; yet, about the contents there is something mousey—the colour perhaps. The fact is, they are disappointing. The letters they contain—a bare third of which are by Jane Welsh—were all written between the middle of 1821 and the end of 1826—that is to say, before either Jane or Carlyle had found themselves. At his best, Carlyle was not a letter-writer; he was a clever man who wrote letters. These have sometimes the personal quality of a good essay, never the charm of familiar correspondence. In these early days his mind is as undeveloped as his style; he is crude, awkward, over-emphatic; apter at catching the faults than the excellences of the eighteenth-century prose writers. That one should write to please rather than to improve one's correspondent was an idea which seems hardly to have occurred to him:

> "When I sit down to write Letters to people I care anything for, I am too apt to get into a certain ebullient humour, and so to indite great quantities of nonsense, which even my own judgment condemns—when too late for being mended."

That is his own admission. Here is a specimen of his solemn admonitions to his future wife:

> "I very much approve your resolution to exercise your powers in some sort of literary effort; and I shall think myself happy, if by any means I can aid you in putting it in practice. There is nothing more injurious to the faculties than to sit poring over books continually without attempting to exhibit any of our own conceptions. We amass ideas, it is true; but at the same time we proportionally weaken our powers of expressing them; a power equally valuable with that of conceiving them, and which, tho' in some degree like it the gift of Nature, is in a far higher degree the fruit of art, and so languishes more irretrievably by want of culture," etc.

Even when writing to a lady with whom one is on the most delicate terms such austerity is excessive, especially when it runs into a dozen pages. Carlyle is at his best when describing people, and it is to be regretted that his editor, out of respect for the memory of Campbell's widow and others long since deceased, has felt obliged to suppress more than one passage in which contemporaries are freely handled. He is at his worst when writing, and generally complaining, about himself; and, like the majority of people who take themselves very seriously, most amusing when unconsciously so. In the October of 1824 he visited Paris and told Miss Welsh just what he thought of it:

> "[I am] daily growing more and more contemptuous of Paris, and the *manière d'être* of its people. Poor fellows! I feel alternately titillated into laughter and shocked to the verge of horror at the hand they make of Life.... Their houses are not houses, but places where they sleep and dress; they live in *cafés* and promenades and theatres; and ten thousand dice are set a-rattling every night in every quarter of their city. Every thing seems gilding and fillagree, addressed to the eye, not to the touch."

Mrs. Carlyle, on the other hand, had a genuine gift; her genius may be small, but it is undeniable. She was never in the first flight of letter-writers, a tiny band which consists, we take it, of Mérimée, Mme. de Sévigné, Horace Walpole, Byron, and whom else? But in that larger second class, the class of Gray and Julie de Lespinasse, Lady Mary Montagu, Swift, Flaubert, Leopardi, Charles Lamb, Gibbon, Fitzgerald, Voltaire, Cicero we suppose, and a good many more, she is entitled to a place. Jane Welsh, however, is by no means Mrs. Carlyle. She was but twenty-five when she married. Here we find her rather too conscious of her own superiority; not only was she the beauty, she was also the Muse of the village; had she been less vain she must have been unnatural. Yet, under all her pert provincialism, we can detect that mysterious quality which distinguishes the good letter-writer. She writes to please two people—her correspondent and herself; she has no need, therefore, to canvass general truths, but can afford to be personal and charming. Her artful wit gives pith and moment to the most trivial enterprises, and turns domestic projects into adventures of high romance. She never makes great things small by declamation; she prefers to make small things great by insinuation. Her friend is assumed to be interested in all that concerns herself, so she is not afraid to be intimate; and a correspondent both clever and intimate is one of those things that make life precious. In a word, her letters (which, to our dismay, besides occupying a bare third of the two volumes, are towards the end disastrously affected by the style of her lover) succeed in giving a whimsical view of her ordinary and external life, viewed from standpoints above and beyond the reach of externals—the head and the heart. Her account of the affair with Mr. Dugald G—— is, in its way, a little masterpiece, but too long for quotation. We select a shorter specimen of her style:

"Such a week I spent in Galloway! There was no amusement within doors, and the weather precluded the chance of finding any without. 'Cœlebs in Search of a Wife' was the only book in the house, and even that was monopolized by a young lady who came to my Uncle's (I strongly suspect) on Cœleb's errand. The rest of us had no weapon of any sort to combat time with, and for four whole days I sat counting the drops of rain that fell from the ceiling into a bowl beneath, or in burbling the chain of my watch for the pleasure of undoing it. 'Oh, Plato! what tasks for a philosopher!' At length in a frenzy of ennui I mounted a brute of a horse that could do nothing but trot, and rode till I was ready to drop from the saddle—just for diversion. I left my companions wondering when it would be fair; and when I returned they were still wondering. How very few people retain their faculties in rainy weather!"

We can hardly make evident by short quotations the difference between the letters of a gifted person and of one who had a gift for letter-writing; the reader, however, who will be at pains to take Lamb's correspondence from the shelf and compare his letters with those of Mrs. Carlyle will no doubt discover what it is that they both possess and Carlyle lacks. We would say, if permitted once again to trot out the weary and well-fired hack, that you may think of Carlyle writing his "Frederick" in a tail-coat, or whatever costume you prefer, and feel sure, if your mind be not too literal, that his letters were written in the same full dress. Far pleasanter to imagine Jane Welsh, coming home from a rout, slipping a gay dressing-gown over a satin petticoat, and gossiping till the fire burnt low. What is more, before she had the privilege of "doing for" a great man with a Scotch sense of economy and a peasant's notion of wifely duties, she may often have so gossiped. The fact is, Carlyle, in his most playful moments, kept one eye on "the eternities," and Jane, in her most solemn, never lost sight of the comic spirit.

The volumes before us are well printed on good paper, and without are embellished by a device—two hearts, stamped in gold, linked with a golden ring, and supported by a plump little cupid; the same device is repeated on the title-page in mauve. Trifles may be significant; whether this symbol was suggested by the editor, or whether the editor was influenced by it, are questions deserving thought. Turning to matters less subtle, we wish that Mr. Alexander Carlyle had not found it necessary to rake up the ashes which reticence had allowed to grow cold. Also, we wish that he had adopted some other policy towards Jane Welsh; the pin, even between deft fingers, is an ignoble and unattractive weapon. In his notes he contrives a small and unpleasant sensation (vol. i, p. 319) which would be more effective were it supported by anything better than a piece of gossip, for which no authority is given, and the doubtful interpretation of one passage in a letter. We are grateful to him, however, for translating all the Latin, French, German, Italian, and Scotch words, and for several touches of unconscious humour, of which the following is a pleasant example:

> "Pen (from Penfillan, home of Miss Welsh's paternal grandfather) was her pet name used to distinguish her from the Welshes of her maternal grandfather's household, especially from her mother's younger sister, whose name was also Jeannie Welsh. Conscious of procrastinating too long in writing, Miss Welsh here sportively enlarges Pen not into Penfillan, but into Penelope, the name of Ulysses' faithful wife, who put off so long the hateful task of choosing a husband from the wasteful and riotous horde of suitors assembled in her house during Ulysses' protracted absence. See Homer's 'Odyssey.'"

FOOTNOTE:

[8] "The Love-Letters of Thomas Carlyle and Jane Welsh." Edited by Alexander Carlyle. 2 vols. Illustrated. (John Lane.)

"Carlyle's First Love, Margaret Gordon, Lady Bannerman." By Raymond Clare Archibald. (John Lane.)

THE LYSISTRATA[9]

Αι Χάριτες τέμένός τι λαβεῖν ὅπερ οὐχὶ πεσεῖται
ζητοῦσαι ψυχὴν εὗρον Ἀριστοφάνους.
[Greek: Ahi Charites temenos ti labein hoper ouchi
peseitai zêtousai psuchên euron Aristophanous.]

PLATO.

Athenæum Jan. 1912

To Plato it seemed that the Graces, seeking an imperishable temple, discovered the soul of Aristophanes. To the grocers and statesmen of Queen Victoria it seemed otherwise. Their taste was a good deal nicerζητοῦσαι ψυχὴν Αριστοφάνους than that of Plato, or of Shakespeare for that matter, or of Dante, Rabelais, Catullus, Voltaire,[10] Gibbon or Balzac, to say nothing of St. Chrysostom (who could not sleep without an Aristophanes under his pillow) or the author of "The Song of Solomon." They did not like vulgarity and they put a stop to it: also in that age *Punch* and the *Times* flourished. What is decent or indecent, vulgar or refined, is, of course, a matter of taste; and each age has a taste of its own. The taste of Athens in her prime, or of Rome in hers, of Italy in the days of Dante or of Raphael, of the court of Elizabeth, or of eighteenth-century France was not the taste of Victorian England. And the strange thing is that, though not only in the arts, but in all the delicacies of life—in personal relations, in sentiment and wit—the great poets, artists and critics are admitted to have been more subtle and fastidious than most curates or tradesmen, in the matter of morals the curates and tradesmen are allowed to know better. In this one respect their sensibilities are to be preferred; in all others they modestly confess themselves inferior to the greatest minds of the ages. Things that seemed beautiful or interesting or amusing to Shakespeare or Plato, to Chaucer or Aristophanes, they know, for certain, to be evil. And since they are evil they are not to be mentioned; discussion of them even— since they are quite sure that they are evil—is a crime. Now the prevention of crime is a duty of the state; so very few of the world's great masterpieces could have been published for the first time in modern England; and it has been impossible for Mr. Bickley Rogers to give us even a translation of the *Lysistrata*.

Were Aristophanes alive and publishing now, not only would his plays be vetoed by the Censor for indelicacy, and boycotted by the libraries, he would be in personal danger on another account; for a judge of the High Court could surely be found to sentence the author of *The Birds* to six months' hard labour for blasphemy. Mr. Rogers, therefore, who made this translation, not in the Athens of Plato, but in the London of Podsnap—in 1878, to be exact—is not much to be blamed for having allowed it to bear the mark of its age. Nevertheless, though pardonable, his compromise is deplorable, since it robs this translation of precisely that quality which gives to most of the others their high importance. For Mr. Rogers is one of those who during the last five-and-twenty years have been busy awakening us to a new sense of the possibilities of life. His share in that task has been to express and restate, in a form appreciable by the modern mind, some of the adventures and discoveries of the Hellenic genius. He is one of those scholars who, consciously or unconsciously, have joined hands with the boldest spirits of the age, and, by showing what the Greeks thought and felt, have revealed to us new worlds of thought and feeling. Now, to write like the sociologists, the subject of the *Lysistrata* is the fundamental nature and necessity of the interdependence of the sexes. But what Aristophanes thought and felt about the matter is just what we shall not find in this translation. For instance, the scene between Cinesias and Myrrhina is essential to a perfect understanding of the play, but the latter part of it (ll. 905-60) is not so much as paraphrased here. And so the spirit languishes; it could flourish only in the body created for it by the poet, and that body has been mutilated.

This version, then, fails to bring out the profound, comic conception that gives unity and significance to the original; nevertheless, it has something more than such literary interest as may be supposed to belong to any work by Mr. Rogers. The comic poet offers matter worthy the consideration of politicians and political controversialists, and this the translator has rendered fearlessly and well. For the *Lysistrata* is a political play, and cannot be discussed profitably apart from its political ideas and arguments. It can no more be treated as pure literature than the poetry of Keats can be treated as anything else. Frankly "pacificist," and to some extent "feminist," hostile, at any rate, to arrogant virility, it sounds in its ideas and arguments oddly familiar to modern ears; and, in the interest of those ears, it may be worth pausing a moment to consider the circumstances in which it was produced.

Some eighteen months earlier—towards the end of 413 B.C.—had come news of the most stunning disaster that was to befall Athens till the final catastrophe at Aegospotami. The greatest armament ever assembled by a Greek state had been annihilated, literally, before Syracuse: the city, itself, was in danger. For that not the less was Aristophanes permitted to produce in the state theatre at the public cost his fiercely anti-militarist and anti-imperialist play. Was it the best, or one of the two or three best, comedies of the year? That was what the Athenians wanted to know. If it was, of course it ought to be presented.

During this long and horrible war (it lasted twenty-eight years), power, as was to be expected, slipped into the hands of vile and violent demagogues, of men who by rhetoric and intrigue induced the people more than once to reject on fair occasions reasonable terms, who in 420, guided by Alcibiades, contrived by an infamous stratagem to upset the Peace of Nicias, and by a combination of evil motives—private interest, public vanity, vindictiveness, greed, and sentimentality—prolonged the war until it ended in the ruin of the city and the irreparable debasement of ancient civilization. These men, as may be supposed, were the butts of our poet's bitterest satire and most furious invective. Yet even they, though incessantly attacked and exposed, never succeeded in prohibiting, and perhaps never wished to prohibit, the performance of his plays.

It has been said that Athens attempted to impose her civilization on the Hellenic world and became barbarous in the attempt. There is, of course, much truth in this. To wage war successfully a state must make itself to some extent barbarous; and the Peloponnesian War ended the progressive phase of Greek culture. The state conquered by Rome was something unrecognizably inferior to the state that Pericles so recklessly jeopardized; and it is interesting to note that the conquest of Greece by Rome did far more for the spread of Greek civilization and culture than any of those projects of aggrandizement and expansion so artfully devised by Athenian imperialists. No reader of Thucydides can doubt that as the struggle intensified Athenian civility diminished: yet, when we remember that even in the throes of war the right of the individual to live and speak freely was not lost, that, on the contrary, during the war, came forth some of the finest and freest criticism with which the world has ever been blest, we shall incline to suspect that even in her decline Athens was decidedly more civilized than most states at their apogee.

Ὁ δε ἀνεξέταστος βίος οὐ βιωτὸς [Greek: ho de anexetastos bios ou biôtos], said Socrates—a life unsifted is a life unspent. Because the Athenians really believed this, because they saw dimly that good states of mind, not wealth nor comfort nor power nor prestige—which are but means—but states of mind, which alone are good in themselves, are the proper end of existence, they refused to sacrifice individual liberty to any god of efficiency. It was to the mind of the individual they looked for absolute good: the state was but a means. Therefore at Athens, after twenty years of stultifying war, the right of the individual to free expression and self-development was scrupulously respected. In this truly liberal atmosphere vivid and original characters grew and flourished, thought and felt, and of their thoughts and feelings have left such record as still charms and tantalizes less fortunate generations. This belief in personal liberty, this respect for the individual mind as the sole source of truth and beauty, made possible Athens, a small short-lived state in the distant past, an ideal towards which the best minds are ever looking back, the glory and grand achievement of the Western world.[11]

Our enthusiasm for that Athenian spirit, which respected art and gave free rein to criticism even at the most desperate moment of the city's history, has carried us a little, but only a little, away from the matter in hand—the political ideas of the *Lysistrata*. Political wisdom, like human folly, seems to obey a law known to men of science as "the Conservation of Energy"—quantity and quality are permanent, form alone changes. It is the Aristophanic method that differs so greatly from that of most modern satirists. For Aristophanes does not confine himself to driving the blade of his wit into the rotten parts of a bad case; he does not score intellectual points only. His method is more fundamental. A clever controversialist can always find joints in the harness of his foe. When Mr. Shaw meets Mr. Belloc in public controversy it is hard to say which makes the greater number of hits. Even harder is it to say that the cause of truth has been much advanced. One may hold, fairly enough, that both sides have been made ludicrous; but it is still fairer to admit that neither has been utterly discredited. If Aristophanes never succeeded in ruining a party, at least he succeeded in discrediting some pestilent opinions. This he did, not so much by a brisk display of intellectual handiness, as by showing that a pompous superstructure was baseless. He makes us feel a position to be absurd, instead of merely thinking certain things in it silly.

The superior, sneering official has not escaped shrewd knocks from the wits of every age. There is a type of mind which, under every form of government, pushes to the front by sheer lack of virtue. Wherever life has become sufficiently mechanical to support a bureaucracy, there will the Poloniuses and Shallows gather, and, wherever there is an official caste, there will be satirists or torture-chambers.[12] Yet, though the self-complacent magistrate has been the butt of the ages, Aristophanes and Shakespeare, and perhaps Flaubert, have alone revealed his essential nullity, because they alone have looked for something essential beneath the accidental. Nothing could be simpler than the character of Polonius; nothing could be more subtle. A rap here, a stab there, and the soul of a minister is exposed. We have come to see, we scarcely know how, that, if he ever had one, he has lost it. Some idea of the simplicity and subtlety of the Aristophanic method may be gathered from the following scene, but to illustrate the extravagance and beauty of the form, or the profundity of the conception, no quotation can suffice. Lysistrata has unfolded her famous scheme for stopping the war: there is to be a sympathetic strike; the women of all the combatant states, principals and allies, are to withhold their services until the war has been stopped:

LYSISTRATA [*ending a speech*]. Then shall the people revere us and honour us,

givers of Joy, and givers of Peace.

MAGISTRATE. Tell us the mode and the means of your doing it.

LYS. First we will stop the disorderly crew,

Soldiers in arms promenading and marketing.

STRATYLLIS [*leader of the chorus of women*]. Yea, by divine Aphrodite, 'tis true.

LYS. Now in the market you see them like Corybants,

jangling about with their armour of mail.

Fiercely they stalk in the midst of the crockery,

sternly parade by the cabbage and kail.

MAG. Right, for a soldier should always be soldierly!

LYS. Troth, 'tis a mighty ridiculous jest,

Watching them haggle for shrimps in the market-place,

grimly accoutred with shield and with crest.

*   *   *   *   *

STRAT. Comes, like a Tereus, a Thracian irregular,

shaking his dart and his target to boot;

Off runs a shopgirl, appalled at the sight of him,

down he sits soldierly, gobbles her fruit.

MAG. You, I presume, could adroitly and gingerly

settle this intricate, tangled concern:

> You in a trice could relieve our perplexities.

LYS. Certainly.

MAG. How? permit me to learn.

LYS. Just as a woman, with nimble dexterity,

> thus with her hands disentangles a skein.

> *　　*　　*　　*　　*

MAG. Wonderful, marvellous feats, not a doubt of it,

> you with your skeins and your spindles can show;
>
> Fools! do you really expect to unravel a
>
> terrible war like a bundle of tow?

LYS. Ah, if you only could manage your politics

> just in the way that we deal with a fleece!

> *　　*　　*　　*　　*

MAG. Heard any ever the like of their impudence,

> these who have nothing to do with the war,
>
> Preaching of bobbins, and beatings, and washing-tubs?

LYS. *Nothing to do with it*, wretch that you are?

The women conclude that one who talks thus is no better than a dead man; and when he sets out on some trusty platitude concerning women's sphere and the married state with

Truly whoever is able to wed—

Lysistrata takes him up sharply with

Truly, old fellow,'tis time you were dead.

Accordingly they prepare with sacrificial pigs, funeral cakes, fillets and chaplets to give the walking corpse a decent burial. The magistrate stumps off, taking Heaven to witness he never was so insulted in his life, which, as Lysistrata observes, amounts to nothing more than grumbling because they have not laid him out.

Twenty-three centuries are gone since Aristophanes wrote the *Lysistrata*, but the safe official who dismisses with a traditional sneer or a smile the notion that any can manage, save those who have been trained to mismanage, is still with us. Perhaps he has outlived the class whose prejudices and limitations he formerly expressed; but in the days of Aristophanes such a class existed, and it is represented here by the chorus of old gentlemen. In those days the men were not the only fools. Aristophanes had no intention of making out that they were. He was a better artist than party man. He was a comic poet who revealed the essential comedy of all things. The chorus of women, Lysistrata herself, and the other leading ladies, all have their foibles and absurdities; only the chorus of men, who are so keenly alive to them, seem never to guess that there are smuts on the pot. To seek in this age and country a companion for these old fellows would be to insult our Western civilization. Let us invent a purely fantastic character; one who could not sleep at night for fear of Prussians and Social Democrats, who clamoured daily for a dozen Dreadnoughts, conscription, and the head of Mr. Keir Hardie on a charger, and yet spent his leisure warning readers of the daily papers against the danger of admitting to any share of power a sex notorious for its panic-fearfulness, intolerance, and lack of humour; such a one would indeed merit admission to the χορός γερόντων [Greek: choros gerontôn], would be a proper fellow to take his stand ἑξῆς Ἀριστογείτονι [Greek: hexês Aristogeitoni], beside the brave Aristogiton, and πατάξαι τῆσδε γραός τήν γνάθον [Greek: pataxai têsde graos tên gnathon], beat down this "monstrous regiment of women."

Aristophanes was a staunch Conservative, but he disliked a stupid argument wherever he found it. He cared intensely about politics, but he could not easily forget that he was an artist. Neither the men nor the women are tied up and peppered with the small shot of his wit; they are allowed to betray themselves. The art consists in selecting from the mass of their opinions and sentiments what is most significant, and making the magistrate, who speaks for the party, deliver himself of judicious commonplaces. The chorus of wiseacres, the bar-parlour politicians, whom chance or misfortune has led to favour one side rather than the other, are less cautious without being less platitudinous. Their talk is all of "inevitable war" and "stripping for the fray," "vindicating rights," "tyranny" and "traitors," "spoliation," "innovation," and "striking good blows for the cause"; at least it was twenty-three hundred years ago.

Men Chorus.

This is not a time for slumber;
 now let all be bold and free,
Strip to meet the great occasion,
 vindicate our rights with me.
I can smell a deep, surprising
Tide of Revolution rising,
Odour as of folk devising
 Hippias's tyranny.
And I feel a dire misgiving,
Lest some false Laconians, meeting
 in the house of Cleisthenes,

Have inspired these wretched women
 all our wealth and pay to seize.
Pay from whence I get my living.
Gods! to hear these shallow wenches
 taking citizens to task,
Prattling of a brassy buckler,
 jabbering of a martial casque!
Gods! to think that they have ventured
 with Laconian men to deal,
Men of just the faith and honour
 that a ravening wolf might feel!
Plots they're hatching, plots contriving,
 plots of rampant Tyranny;
But o'er US they shan't be Tyrants,
 no, for on my guard I'll be,
And I'll dress my sword in myrtle,

and with firm and dauntless hand,

Here beside Aristogeiton

resolutely take my stand,

Marketing in arms beside him.

This the time and this the place

When my patriot arm must deal a

—blow upon that woman's face.

One is tempted to quote Mr. Rogers indefinitely; indeed, there are a score of good things to which we would gladly call attention. Having warned readers that this version is not a translation in the sense that the versions of *The Frogs* and *The Birds* are, we can, with a clear conscience, urge all to read it who care for good literature or are interested in political ideas. They will not be disappointed; only, we would suggest to those whose Greek has grown a little rusty that a literal translation in French or German would be a suitable companion for the English paraphrase. Without it, they will hardly understand what provoked Plato's splendid compliment and would bring down upon the author, were he alive, the rigours of our English law.

FOOTNOTES:

[9] "The Lysistrata of Aristophanes, acted at Athens in the year B.C. 411." The Greek Text Revised, with a Translation into Corresponding Metres, Introduction, and Commentary, by Benjamin Bickley Rogers. (Bell and Sons.)

[10] Voltaire, by the way, was no admirer of Aristophanes. "Ce poète comique," said he, "qui n'est ni comique ni poète, n'aurait pas été admis parmi nous à donner ses farces à la foire Saint-Laurent." But that was not because he was indecent, but because to Voltaire, who said much the same of Shakespeare, he seemed extravagantly incorrect.

[11] Of course this panegyric needs qualification. What panegyric does not? The Athenians condemned Socrates. Yes ... yes. But, as a statement of the general belief and, what is more, the practice of Athens, these rather excited paragraphs may stand.

[12] *Note*: 1918. Though assuredly our satirists hide their light under a bushel, the tiny flickers do not escape the eyes of our officials. Let them beware. In 415, after the mutilation of the Hermae, there was a panic at Athens and a reign of terror instigated by some of the demagogues. Torture, though contrary to the laws of Athens and to all Athenian sentiment, was proposed. The proposal was accepted; but when the

moment for execution came the *ecclesia*—the mass meeting of citizens, that is to say—refused to allow it. Now Pericles would never have proposed such a thing; neither would Mr. Asquith: but suppose in these days some more popular and less responsible leader were to back the project, I wonder whether the English people would decline to follow him.

———————————

TRELAWNY'S LETTERS[13]

Athenæum Jan. 1911

Any one who has read Trelawny's recollections of Shelley and Byron must know that their author was something much more considerable than a friend of the great. Any one who, lured by that enchanting book, has gone on to the "Adventures of a Younger Son" may be pardoned for supposing, if we are really to take it for autobiography, that its author was a stupendous liar. Just what he was—the man who wrote those enthralling memoirs and that excellent romance—may now be pretty well made out from this collection of old and new letters put together by Mr. Buxton Forman.

"Vigour and directness," "transparent honesty and complete fearlessness," are the qualities that impress this able editor as he reads the letters of the man who, in his opinion, "was less tainted with the sordid commercialism and ever-increasing snobbery of that century [the nineteenth] than almost any man one could name as having lived through so large a part of it." We agree heartily; but, of course, there is more to be said—for instance, that Trelawny sometimes reminds us of an extraordinarily intelligent schoolboy, at others of a rather morbid minor poet. Only, the vitality of few schoolboys amounts almost to genius, and minor poets are not always blest with feelings fundamentally sound. Most of his vices were the defects of good qualities. A powerful imagination may be fairly held accountable for his habit of romancing, and a brave vocabulary for some of his exaggeration. His vanity and violence—as childish as his love of mystery, and often as childishly displayed—were forms in which his high spirits and passionate nature expressed themselves. Art, in the shape of a bad education, aggravated his faults; but his honesty and imagination, his generosity and childlike capacity for admiration and affection were from nature alone. He was a schoolboy who never grew up; cultivating his cabbages at Worthing in 1875, he is essentially the same shrewd, passionate, romantic scapegrace who deserted his ship in Bombay harbour soon after the battle of Trafalgar, and burnt Shelley's body on the foreshore at Via Reggio.

Like all boys, Trelawny was exceedingly impressionable, and at the beginning of this book we find him under the influence of the learned ladies of Pisa. Left to himself, he wrote with point and vigour prose as rich in colour and spirit as it is poor in grammar and spelling. His letter to the

Literary Gazette, published in this volume, is a good example of his narrative style. But even his style could be perverted:

> "I must give you the consolation of knowing—that you have inflicted on me indiscribable tortures—that your letter has inflicted an incurable wound which is festering and inflaming my blood—and my pride and passion, warring against my ungovernable love, has in vain essayed to hide my wounded feelings—by silently submitting to my evil destiny."

So he wrote to Claire Clairmont in December 1822; but under the language of the minor romantic throbs the lusty passion of a man.

Shelley's influence was great; with him Trelawny was always natural and always at his best; but Shelley was a wizard who drew the pure metal from every ore. With Byron it was different. Trelawny was almost as vain as "the Pilgrim of Eternity," as sensitive, and, when hurt, as vindictive. He was jealous of Byron's success with women—they were two of a trade—and especially of his relations with Claire. When Byron posed Trelawny posed, and when the one sulked the other sulked; but was any man except Shelley big enough to brook his lordship's moods? That Byron valued Trelawny is certain; he invited him to Greece because he knew his worth. Once arrived, Byron had the wit to perceive that Mavrocordato, albeit the meanest of masters, was the best and most serviceable to be had at the moment. Trelawny, as was to be expected, fell under the spell of Odysseus, at that time in more or less open revolt against the provisional government, but an adventurer of fierce and reckless spirit, in manner and appearance a romantic outlaw, a man after his own heart. Henceforth Byron is reckoned at best a dupe, and at worst a sluggish poltroon; while Trelawny, it is said, imitated his hero so loyally that "he ate, dressed, and even spat in his manner." When the poet died Trelawny spoke with characteristic feeling:

> "With all his faults I loved him truly.... If it gave me pain witnessing his frailties, he only wanted a little excitement to awaken and put forth *virtues* that redeemed them all."

But the iron had entered into his soul, old sores rankled, he could not forgive; to the last he was willing to pay back his rival in his own coin—sneers and abuse.

As Trelawny could scarcely write to a woman without making love to her, and as his relations with Mary Shelley were necessarily emotional and intimate, an ambiguous proposal and a handful of affectionate letters will not persuade us that he ever cared more seriously for her than for scores of others. Though some letters must have been written when he was courting the sister of Odysseus or keeping a harem at Athens, and others when his heart was disengaged, can any one decide which are sincere and which are not? Or, rather, are they not all equally sincere? The following extract may help us to a conclusion:

> "I say! the poet [Shelley] was a thorough mormon—why did he not declare himself and anticipate the sect? I would have joined him and found him a settlement—it would not hold together without a superstition—for man all over the world are [*sic*] superstitious—it's the nature of the animal—your mother was a simpleton to have never heard of a man being in love with two women; when we are young we are in love with all women—the bible would call it by its proper name, lust."

So wrote Trelawny in 1869 (he had recovered his style) to Claire Clairmont. His letters to her, now published for the first time, compose the largest and liveliest part of the volume. If he cared for one woman more than another, we believe that woman was Claire. She was not good, but she has been more than sufficiently reviled. For Trelawny that she was beautiful sufficed; let it satisfy the vindictiveness of virtue that she suffered horribly. What precisely was the degree of their intimacy is not clear; but, in view of Claire's reputation and certain passages in these letters, it is perhaps not unfair to suppose that at any rate for a short time in the year 1822 she was his mistress. Be that as it may, after Shelley's death they parted, and doubtless it will be said she treated her lover ill. To us it appears that he gave as good as he got. She was mercenary, and he was inconstant. If we read Letter XX aright, when she did offer, after some months of prudent dalliance, to live with him at Florence, he replied that he had but £500 a year, which was not enough for two. An establishment on the confines of respectability was the last thing he desired. Neither ever loved truly; but Trelawny, for a time, felt violent physical passion for the woman whose head and shoulders remind us of what dealers call a Giorgione. Such is the story, so far as we can deduce it from these letters; each, if our conjecture serve, was partially satisfied, for in money matters Trelawny always treated his lady handsomely, though he could not or would not give her what most she wanted—material security.

He never lost his taste for Claire; and on the ruins of their bitter and agitated relations was built a kind of friendship, in which expansion and intimacy and malice were all possible, and which is aptly commemorated by these vivid and entertaining letters. As for Mary, her character deteriorated and Trelawny's judgment grew more acute. Her corners grew more brutally protuberant beneath the tissue of glamour cast over them by a name. To her also Trelawny's purse was open; but long before the quarrel over

"Queen Mab" his generous spirit had begun to groan under her prim banality, and to express itself in ungenerous backbitings. His final estimate he imparted to Claire when he was seventy-eight years old, and it remains for those who dislike to disprove it:

> "Mary Shelley's jealousy must have sorely vexed Shelley—indeed she was not a suitable companion for the poet—his first wife Harriett must have been more suitable—Mary was the most conventional slave I ever met—she even affected the pious dodge, such was her yearning for society—she was devoid of imagination and Poetry—she felt compunction when she had lost him— she did not understand or appreciate him."

There are two big gaps in the correspondence with Claire: one from 1838 to 1857, the other from 1857 to 1869. At the age of seventy-seven we find Trelawny still unchanged: "All my early convictions and feelings harden with my bones—age has not tamed or altered me." He had lived through the wildest adventures: in a cave on Mount Parnassus he had been shot through the body and had pardoned one of his assailants; he had swum the rapids below Niagara; he had played the pirate in the South Seas and flirted with Mrs. Norton in Downing Street; and now, a veteran and something of a lion, he astonished London parties with his gasconade and the Sussex fisher-folk with his bathing exploits. We can believe that his conversation was "brilliant," but "most censorious"; his letters to Claire give some idea of it: "Women have taken to gin—men have always done so, now it's women's turn"; "—— is as gross and fat as —— and from the same cause—gluttony and sotting—it's all the fashion."

And here we would interpose a query—Was it really necessary to suppress the names? This elaborate and unscholarly tenderness for the feelings of the friends and relations of the dead, and for those of their descendants even, is becoming, in our judgment, a nuisance. Had people been so fussy and timid always we should have no history worth reading. After all, men, and women too for that matter, have got to stand on their own feet. We are not our grandmothers' keepers. No one will think at all the worse of Mr. Smith because some lively diarist has hinted that his great maiden aunt was no such thing: neither will any one think much the worse of the old lady. Besides, it is easy for Mr. Smith to say that the diarist was a liar who couldn't possibly have known anything about it. The past belongs to the present, and the dead are in some sort public property. It is not well, we think, that history should be impoverished, and an instrument of culture blunted, out of regard for the feelings of stray nephews and nieces, and we commend to editors and biographers the saying of that undergraduate who to his friend's complaint—"Hi, Johnnie, you've shot my father," replied, with a truly British sense of give and take—"Never mind, have a shot at mine."

Poor Claire became devout in old age and provoked a comprehensive growl from Shelley's untamed friend: "I am not one of that great sect whose vanity, credulity, and superstition makes them believe in God—the devil—souls and immortality." Yet with what cheerful wisdom he laughs away the fancy, which threatened to become an obsession, that Allegra was still alive in 1869: "My dear Clare, you may be well in body; but you have a bee in your bonnet." He suggests raking up "some plausible cranky old dried-up hanger-on" of fifty-two or so, who "should follow you about like a feminine Frankenstein," as he carelessly puts it. He tried to mitigate the crazy malevolence she cherished for her earliest lover: "Your relentless vindictiveness against Byron is not tolerated by any religion that I know of"; while through the rack of jibes, malisons, and ebullitions of wilfulness shines steadily his veneration for the great poet he loved:

> "You say he [Shelley] was womanly in some things—so
> he was, and we men should all be much better if we had a
> touch of their feeling, sentiment, earnestness, and
> constancy; but in all the best qualities of man he excelled."

Through these letters—through all Trelawny's writings—runs a wonderful sense of power. He was not one to seek out the right word or prune a sentence; his strength is manifest in his laxities. He believed that no task, intellectual or physical, was beyond him; so he wrote as he swam, taking his ease, glorying in his vitality, secure in a reserve of strength equal to anything. A sense of power and a disregard for syntax—these are his literary characteristics. He read Shakespeare and Shelley, and it is not clear that he cared greatly for much besides; he liked Swinburne, and was profoundly interested in Darwin. Late in life he discovered Blake and was fascinated. What Trelawny cared for in literature was Imagination, the more sublime the better, while in life he had a taste for Truth and Freedom. He was always something of an oddity. He loathed superstition, cant and snobbery and said so in a way that gave much pain to the nicest people. He was of that disconcerting sort which, excelling in all that ordinary people admire, admires, for its part, what they hate—the abnormal and distinguished. He was a man of action who mistrusted common sense, a good fellow on the side of cranks: the race has never been common and is now almost extinct.

FOOTNOTE:

[13] "Letters of Edward John Trelawny." Edited, with a brief Introduction and Notes, by H. Buxton Forman. (Frowde.)

SOPHOCLES IN LONDON

I

"Œdipus" at Covent Garden

Athenæum Jan. 1912

There need be nothing anachronous or archæological about a performance of *Œdipus* at Covent Garden. There is no reason why the plays of Sophocles should move us less than they moved the Athenians twenty-three hundred years ago, and there is some for supposing that we, who live in the twentieth, are more likely to appreciate them than those who lived in any intervening century. For everywhere to-day is a cry for simplicity and significance, and art more simple and significant than the Attic drama does not exist. In less than ten thousand words Sophocles tells all that can be told about a terrible and complex tragedy. Zola or Meredith in ten times the space would have added nothing. They would only have put flesh on bone and muscle; they would have given us trappings and ornament where Sophocles gives nothing but bare springs and forces.

Yet in this flat, lean, Attic drama all Latin realism and Celtic romance, all details and suggestions, are implicit. It states just those fundamental things of which all the rest are but manifestations or consequences. There is as much psychology in the scene between Œdipus and Jocasta, a matter of some seventy lines, as could be forced into seventy pages by a modern novelist. A change of feeling that it would take Mr. Henry James a chapter to elaborate is indicated by a statement, a question, and a reply. Sophocles could never be satisfied with anything short of the essential: that he stated; the rest he left out.

Though Prof. Gilbert Murray is, as every one knows, a charming and sensitive scholar, he is not the ideal translator of Sophocles. Perhaps the Zolas and Merediths—especially the Merediths—impress him too easily; perhaps he loves too well the literary tradition, the European tradition of five hundred years, to understand that the greatest poetry is rarely poetical:

A Voice, a Voice, that is borne on the Holy Way!

What art thou, O Heavenly One, O Word of the Houses of Gold?

Thebes is bright with thee, and my heart it leapeth; yet is it cold,

And my spirit faints as I pray.

I—ê! I—ê!

What task, O Affrighter of Evil, what task shall thy people essay?

One new as our new-come affliction,

Or an old toil returned with the years?

Unveil thee, thou dread benediction,

Hope's daughter and Fear's.

This is very pretty, but is it Sophocles?—or Swinburne? Still, grace there is, and distinction, in all that Prof. Murray writes—qualities that are not accentuated by the mouthings of the protagonist, Mr. Martin Harvey, the uninspired drone of the chorus, or the intermittent shrieking and bawling of the crowd. In the translation of the Professor the simple profundities of the poet become delicate verse, which in the mouth of the histrion is turned into rhythmless rhetoric.

But, after all, in performances of this sort it is not the play, but the production, that is the thing—though that is less true of this than of any other Reinhardt entertainment we have yet seen. Still, deeds not words: it is by theatrical effects and stage decoration, if by any means, that the message of Sophocles is to be conveyed to the people of London. That both are remarkable cannot be denied. *Œdipus* is a fine show. It is erudite, striking, and ingenious; but it is not a work of art. What is it, then? To borrow an expressive, though unnecessarily insulting term from our neighbours, it is "Le faux bon."

And what is "Le faux bon"? It is something exceedingly difficult to produce. We do not wish to belittle it; we wish to make plain its nature. If we succeed, we shall show also how choice and rare a thing this *Œdipus* is. At any rate, it keeps good company. The plays of Mr. Stephen Phillips are classical examples of the "faux bon," and, to remove a suspicion of disparagement, we hasten to add that the plays of M. Rostand and FitzGerald's paraphrase of Omar are examples too. The brilliant and entertaining pictures of Mr. Nicholson and Mr. Orpen serve our purpose even better, so closely do they resemble the first-rate. And now in this, the latest art, the new art of the theatre, come M. Bakst with his *Scheherazade*, and Prof. Reinhardt with *Sumurun* and *The Miracle*, levying contribution on all the others, culling from them all those features that people of taste expect and recognize in a work of art.

For "le faux bon" is produced to meet the demands of a tasteful and cultivated society—a society that knows as much about art as can be taught. People who have been brought up on terms of familiarity with the arts learn to recognize all those features that a work of art ought to possess; they know the effects that it ought to produce; but, unless born with the power of reacting emotionally and directly to what they see and hear, they cannot understand what a work of art is. Such people are numerous in these days. Far too intelligent to be duped by imitations of particular plays, or poems, or pictures, what they require is imitation art. And that is what they get. In Prof. Reinhardt's productions there are dramatic pauses and suspensions, effects of light and sound, combinations of movement and mass, line and colour, which recall, not particular works, but general ideas based on the study of hundreds of works, and provoke, in the right kind of spectator, precisely those trains of thought and feeling that are provoked by real works of art. True, they express no first-hand emotion, neither does the real thing to lovers of the "faux bon," but they cause physical reactions (as when Jocasta's women rush screaming on to the stage) subtle enough to do duty for æsthetic emotions. It is hard to believe that these refined stimulants are precisely the same in kind as the collisions and avalanches of melodrama; but they are.

Œdipus is a good "show." To appreciate it properly we must realize that it is nothing else. We must compare it with pageants and ballets; and if, so comparing it, we like it less than some that we have seen at the Empire and the Alhambra, the generous will attribute our eccentricity to an overdeveloped moral sense. To be frank, we do not believe that Prof. Reinhardt or M. Bakst has more to say than the creators of our best musical ballets. But, while the latter modestly pretend to nothing more than the flattery of our senses by means of form and sound and colour, the wizards of "the new art" claim to express the most profound and subtle emotions. We prefer "1830" to The Miracle, because it is unpretentious and sincere. We prefer Œdipus to the pantomime because it is prettier and shorter. As works of art they all seem to us about equal.

II

The "Trachiniæ" at "The Court."

Athenæum July 1911

The players of Bedford College are winning for themselves a place of honour amongst those who help the modern world to understand Greek drama. The traditional opinion that the Athenians were a race of fools with a sense of form, who wrote tedious verse to perfection, has been ousted by a new doctrine, less false, but even more dangerous. A race of scholars arose who assumed, reasonably enough, that plays written by intelligent men for an intelligent public could not be quite so dull as tradition proclaimed; and though to rob the classics of their terrors needed much audacity and some irreverence, the new ideas won ground by sheer force of plausibility. Unfortunately, to the modern scholar an intelligent public meant a public of modern scholars. He peopled the Attic theatre with an audience of cultivated liberals, and by "a good play" meant the sort of play such a public would relish. Whence it followed that the Athenian dramatists must have concerned themselves with those problems which have been so acutely discussed in the plays of Mr. Galsworthy and Mr. Shaw.

As a fact, Athenian tragedy is never, or hardly ever, concerned with intellectual matters of any sort; its business is to express emotion, and this it has done in the most perfect literary form ever devised by man. The great merit of Miss E. B. Abraham's performance is that she plays the part of Deianeira neither as if that lady were a relic of the most insipid period of classical sculpture, nor yet as though she were cousin-german to Hedda Gabler. When she errs, she errs on the side of modernity; and that is as it should be. Certainly she puts too much "psychology" into the character of the fond, gentle lady, whose simple humanity at pathetic odds with Fate wins sympathy from the audience without effort or emphasis; while a hankering after the latest subtleties has led her to misunderstand completely the passage (580-95 in the acting edition) in which she supposes the queen to be justifying herself to a reluctant chorus, whereas, in fact, she is justifying herself to the Universe, and giving the audience a hint. The meek chorus is only too willing to agree.

Poor is the triumph of Fate over a timid woman. Heracles is a more splendid but not less helpless victim. Mr. G. Edwards understands the part well. Very fine was the passionate indignation, surging up through physical agony, in the first great speech; and this mood is made to prevail until in the name "Νἐσσος [Greek: Nessos]" the hero recognizes the finger of God. From that point, though violent and dictatorial still to his son and the respectful mortals about him, the tyrant submits sullenly to those he can neither vanquish nor appease.

Mr. Garrod, who played the part of Hyllus, spoke his lines exceedingly well. Perhaps the chorus was a little too classical—that is to say, too stiff and lackadaisical; but the phrasing was always pretty and sometimes unexpected, and the lovely strophe beginning, ὃν αἰόλα νύξ ἐναριζομένα [Greek: hon aiola nux enarizomena;]

seemed to gain a new enchantment from the delicately concerted voices.

Scholars will have to bring strong arguments to justify what is an obvious literary blemish in the distribution of the concluding lines. Somehow or other, between Hyllus and the chorus, the sombre intensity of the complaint was allowed to evaporate. The words,

τὰ δὲ νῦν ἐστῶτ οικτρὰ μὲν ἡμίν,

αἰσχρὰ

[Greek: ta de nun hestôt' oiktra men hêmin,

aischra]

and

κοὐδὲν τούτων ὁ τι μὴ Ζεὺς

[Greek: kouden toutôn o ti mê Zeus]

should come from the same lips, surely.

O Providence, I will not praise,
Neither for fear, nor joy of gain,
Your blundering and cruel ways.

*　　*　　*　　*　　*

And all men's miserable days,
And all the ugliness and pain,
O Providence, I will not praise.

THE FLIGHT OF THE DRAGON[14]

Athenæum Oct. 1911

No one will be surprised to learn that fourteen hundred years ago the Chinese laid down six canons of art. Nothing is more natural than that some great artist, reviewing in old age his life and work, should deduce from the mass of experience and achievement certain propositions, and that these, in time, should become rules, to be preached by pedants, practised by dilettanti, and ignored by every artist worthy of the name. What does surprise us is that the first of these Chinese canons should be nothing less than a definition of that which is essential in all great art. "Rhythmic vitality," Prof. Giles calls it; Mr. Okakura, "the Life-movement of the Spirit through the Rhythm of things"; Mr. Binyon suggests "the fusion of the rhythm of the spirit with the movement of living things."

> "At any rate," he says, "what is certainly meant is that the artist must pierce beneath the mere aspect of the world to seize and himself to be possessed by that great cosmic rhythm of the spirit which sets the currents of life in motion. We should say in Europe that he must seize the universal in the particular."

"The universal in the particular," that is perhaps what the greatest art expresses. Perhaps it is a widespread consciousness of this that produces all great movements; and perhaps the history of their decline and fall is nothing more than a history of its gradual decay and disappearance. Great movements seem to arise when men become aware suddenly that the universe has a soul: the first artists of a movement are the men who perceive most clearly this soul in every part of the universe; they are called Primitives. They are men driven to art by the intolerable necessity of expressing what they feel; they break silence only because they have something to say; and their one object is to say it as completely and intelligibly as possible. Primitives stand in a class by themselves because they have perceived more clearly than others the reality that lies beneath the superficial, and because, having no other end in view, they have expressed it more completely.

Great movements are alike in their beginnings; whether they are Buddhist or Byzantine, Greek or Egyptian, Assyrian or Mexican, their primitives have two qualities in common, profundity and directness. And in their histories, so far as we may judge from the scanty records of ancient civilizations, all have a general resemblance. Always, as the sense of reality decays, the artist labours to conceal under technical proficiency the poverty of his emotional experience. For the inspired artist technique was nothing but a means; for his hungry successors it becomes an end. For the man who has little to say the manner of saying it gains consequence, and in a manner which has been elaborated into an intricate craft the greatest emotions cannot be expressed. The circle is vicious. With the exaltation and elaboration of craftsmanship expression first falls into neglect and then becomes impossible. Those who are not content to marvel at cleverness, but still ask emotion of art, must be satisfied with such as craftsmen can supply. If pictures no longer express feeling they may at least provoke it. If painting is to be a mere question of pattern-making, at least let the patterns be pretty. Sensuous beauty and cunning delineation become rivals for the throne whence expression has been ousted. So, with occasional irregularities, the path winds down the hill. Skill itself declines, and the sense of beauty runs thin. At the bottom, for what once was art—the expression of man's most holy emotions—smart tradesmen offer, at fancy prices, mechanical prettiness, cheap sentiment, and accurate representation.

Comparisons between the history of Asiatic and of European art are admittedly possible; but as yet we believe the precise nature of the similarity has not been stated. It lies in the fact that both conform to the general laws of decay. The Asiatic movement with which we are familiar is essentially Buddhist; it expresses that sense of the universe that is expressed in another form by Buddhist doctrine and its later developments along the lines of Taoist idealism. How far the spread of Buddhism in China represents a spiritual reaction from the dry materialism of Confucianism is no matter for brief and dogmatic discussion. We need only say that the fourth-century painting in the British Museum by Ku K'ai-chih, though the artist himself is said to have been a Buddhist, belongs clearly to an earlier movement than that of which the T'ang and just pre-T'ang masterpieces are the primitives. By comparison with early Buddhist art this exquisite picture is sufficiently lacking in emotional significance to tempt one to suppose that it represents the ripe and highly cultivated decadence of a movement that the growing religious spirit was soon to displace. Slight as his acquaintance with this early art must be, an Englishman who visited regularly the exhibition at Shepherd's Bush was able to gather from eight or ten pictures, a couple of large wooden Bodhisattvas, and a few small figures in bronze, some idea of the way in which Japanese primitives could enter and express the world of reality. That same power he will find in the Byzantine mosaics of the sixth century, which express the earliest triumphs of another spiritual revolution over the cultured materialism of a moribund civilization.

That new movement spread slowly across Europe, and till the middle of the twelfth century there was no general decline. But the best was over in France before the twelfth century was out. Gothic architecture is juggling in stone and glass. In Italy Giotto followed Cimabue; and Giotto could not always resist the temptation to state the particular and leave the universal out. He sometimes tells us facts instead of expressing emotions. In the full Renaissance the coarsest feeling sufficed to flavour a handsome, well-made picture.

Meanwhile, under the Ming dynasty (1368-1644) Asiatic art had reached much the same stage. The Ming picture in the British Museum known as *The Earthly Paradise* is inferior to the best work of Botticelli, with which it is commonly compared, but reminds us, in its finished grace and gaiety, of a painting by Watteau. Korin, towards the end of the Ming period, is about as empty as Velasquez and more brilliant than Frans Hals. The eighteenth century, one inclines to believe, was the same everywhere. Stylistic obsession and the taste for material beauty ended in mechanical prettiness, altogether inexpressive or sentimental. In both hemispheres painting was reduced to a formula—a formula for producing elegant furniture.

But even in the age of decay Oriental art retained traces of primitive splendour. It never sank into mere representation. The men who turned out the popular Japanese colour-prints, though they chose the same subjects as the Dutch genre painters, were artists enough to treat them differently and to look for something significant beneath the mass of irrelevant accidents. Also they preserved a nicer sensibility to material beauty. A cheap Japanese print has sometimes the quality of a painting by Whistler. Indeed, the superiority of the Orientals is discreetly insinuated from beginning to end of Mr. Binyon's essay. Equal, if not superior, to the Greek or Christian in the primitive stage, the Asiatic movement clung to the heights longer, sank more gradually, and never sank so low. These facts are painful, but patent; they require explanation.

Why is Oriental art generally superior to European? Bearing in mind what has been said about the nature of the greatest art, we shall expect it to be because in the East they have kept in closer touch with reality. That is precisely what has happened. The emotional life has never been in the East what it has become in the West, the rare possession of a fortunate few. There the practical life has been kept subordinate, a means to supporting the emotional. In China men still go about their business that they may purchase leisure in which to contemplate reality. In Europe we are practical; and reality is banished from the life of the practical man who regards all things as means instead of contemplating them as ends. He sees just what is of use to him, and no more. He sees enough for identification and recognition; in fact, he reads the labels on things. The labels are all he requires. In the emotional life things are valued for their significance—for what they are, not for what they can be made to do; they are seen whole because they are seen as ends. The practical man sees only a part—the part that serves his purpose. The camera sees more than that, it sees all the details; but it cannot see the spirit—that has to be felt.

Most Europeans think of boats as means of locomotion, of apples as eatables. They recognize such things by their serviceable qualities; their individuality, the universal in these particulars, escapes them. In a picture of a boat or an apple they look for those unessential qualities which minister to their pleasure, and of which alone they are aware. The cleverness of a man who can paint fruit that tempts urchins impresses them; but the artist who feels, and tries to express, the soul of fruit and flowers they take for an incompetent dunce or a charlatan.

> "One might say that man has been a monarch, looking to his subject-world only for service and for flattery, and just because of this lordly attitude he has failed to understand that subject-world, and, even more, has failed to understand himself."

In the East men have ever set the spiritual life above the practical, and artists have excelled in expressing the very essence of material things because they expressed what they felt, instead of representing what the ordinary man sees. They have felt that if the spirit informs all, then all must have individual significance. To see things as means is to see what is most useful and least important about them. To see things as ends is to be shockingly unpractical; it is to see God in everything; it is to exalt the spirit above the flesh; it is not the way to "get on"; but it is the only way to produce significant art, and, indeed, it is only on such terms that life itself signifies.

So far we have admitted the superiority of the East: the last word has yet to be said. Few observant people will deny that there are signs of an awakening in Europe. The times are great with the birth of some new thing. A spiritual renaissance may be at hand. Meanwhile, we are not suffered to ignore the huge strides in material progress that are the chief glory of modern Japan; nor have we failed to remark that the latest art to reach us from that country proved, when displayed with some ostentation at Shepherd's Bush, equal in vulgarity of sentiment, flashiness of execution, and apelike imitation to the worst that can be seen at Burlington House. Philistinism, it seems, finds ready converts on the other side of the globe. Let the spokesmen of the young and bustling empire be heard. Shiba Kokan, the pupil of Harunobu, says in his "Confessions":

"In Occidental art objects are copied directly from nature; hence before a landscape one feels as if one were placed in the midst of nature. There is a wonderful apparatus called the photograph, which gives a facsimile copy of the object, whatever it is, to which it is directed. Nothing which has not actually been seen is sketched, nor is a nameless landscape reproduced, as we often see done in Chinese productions.... A painting which is not a faithful copy of nature has neither beauty nor is worthy of the name."

And this is the considered judgment of that popular modern painter Okio:

"The use of art is to produce copies of things, and if an artist has a thorough knowledge of the properties of the thing he paints, he can assuredly make a name.... Without the true depiction of objects there can be no pictorial art. Nobility of sentiment and suchlike only come after a successful delineation of the external form of an object."

Such men would be very much at home at an Academy banquet or in the parlour of a suburban stockbroker and less so in the world of art than a saint would be in Wall Street. For whereas the saint would perceive the spark of the universal in the particular stockjobber, the stockjobber and his friends, Mr. Okio, the delineator, and the philophotographic Mr. Kokan, are blind to anything that is not on the surface. Japan, we are told, is to shape the future of the Eastern hemisphere. Japan is "forging ahead." Already she has set her hand to the task of civilizing, that is to say Europeanizing, China—just at the moment when Europe is coming to loathe her own grossness. Time is the master of paradox. Who shall say what surprises are too fantastic for his contriving? Can the classic distinction between East and West, that venerable mother of trite reflections and bad arguments, be, after all, mutable? Is the unchanging East changeable? Is Mr. Kipling's thrilling line no more than the statement of a geographical truism? England they tell us was once a tropical forest; London may yet be the spiritual capital of the world, while Asia—rich in all that gold can buy and guns can give, lord of lands and bodies, builder of railways and promulgator of police regulations, glorious in all material glories—postures, complacent and obtuse, before a Europe content in the possession of all that matters.

FOOTNOTE:

[14] "The Flight of the Dragon: an Essay on the Theory and Practice of Art in China and Japan." By Laurence Binyon. (John Murray.)

WILLIAM MORRIS[15]

New Statesman Oct. 1914

Here is a book that starts a dozen hares, any one of which would be worth catching or hunting, at any rate, through a couple of large-type columns. For a really good book about William Morris is bound to raise those questions that Morris made interesting and his disciples fashionable, and that our children, we may hope, will one day make vital. "How far can society affect art, or art society?" "What might we have made of machinery and what has machinery made of us?" "Was the nineteenth century a disaster or only a failure?" These are the questions that it seems right and natural for a writer who has made William Morris his peg to discuss; and if I discuss something quite different it may look as though, forsaking profitable hares, I were after a herring of my own trailing. Yet, reading this book, I find that the question that interests me most is: "Why does Clutton Brock tend to overrate William Morris?" To answer it I have had to discover what sort of person I suppose Clutton Brock to be, and William Morris to have been.

Clutton Brock is one of our best critics. When I say this, of course I take into consideration his unsigned writings, the anonymity of which is not so strict as to make my judgment indiscreet. Without the subtlety of a philosopher or a trained dialectician, he has been blest with a powerful intellect which enables him, unlike most of our critics, not only to distinguish between sense and nonsense, but himself to refrain from saying what is utterly absurd. Mr. Brock does not like nonsense, and he never talks it. Both the form and the content of his criticism are intellectual. He is in the great English tradition—the tradition of Dryden and Johnson and Macaulay and Leslie Stephen; he has an argumentative prose-style and a distaste for highfalutin, and, where the unenlightened intellectualism of Macaulay and Leslie Stephen, and the incorrigible common sense of Johnson, might have pitched these eminent men into the slough of desperate absurdity, it often happens that Mr. Brock, whose less powerful mind is sweetened by a sense of art, contrives to escape.

No man who has ever done anything worth doing has done less highfalutin than Morris. He was always the craftsman who kept close to his material, and thought more about the block and the chisel than about æsthetic ecstasy. The thrills and ecstasies of life, he seems to have felt, must come as by-products out of doing one's job as well as one could: they were not things, he thought, to aim at, or even talk about overmuch. I do not agree with Morris, but that is beside the point. The point is that Clutton Brock is unwilling to disagree with him violently. He has a peculiar kindness for Morris that does not surprise me. He is a man who works for his living, and does his work so well that we may be sure he wins from it delight. The greater part of what he writes he does not sign; and there are thousands of people in England who, though they hardly know his name, have yet been affected by his mind. As he sits quietly producing a surprising quantity of good literature, he must sometimes feel very near those anonymous craftsmen of the Middle Ages who, lost in the scaffolding, struck out forms that would to-day make only too familiar the names of their creators. At such moments, can he be less than partial to the man who understood so well the greatness and the dignity of those nameless artists?

Morris was amongst the first to perceive that much of the greatest art has been produced anonymously and collectively; and we may be sure that Clutton Brock shares his dislike for that worship of names, that interest in catalogues and biographies, which amongst the collecting classes still does duty for æsthetic sensibility. Morris was indignant, as well he might be, when he heard the pictures of some famous artist—famous because he signed his name and left some record of his life—exalted above the sculpture and windows of Chartres—the work of obscure stone-cutters and verriers. He loved the mediæval craftsmen for the fineness of their work and for their personal modesty. He liked to think of men who could take their orders from a *contre-maître* and execute them superbly, partly, I think, because he saw that these were men who could be fitted into his ideal State. And Mr. Clutton Brock, good Socialist that he is, must, I suppose, himself have been perplexed by that problem which confronts every modern State-projector: What is to be done about the artists? How are these strange, turbulent, individualistic creatures to be fitted into any rational collectivism? What place can be found in Utopia for people who do not work to live, but live to do what they consider their own peculiar piece of work? Now, if only they were craftsmen, they would make what was wanted; they would do what they were told.

Some feeling of this sort may, I think, be at the back of Mr. Clutton Brock's peculiar sympathy with Morris; it would explain, too, why he did less than justice to Shelley in that remarkable study he published some years ago. He could not quite forgive the poet for being so hopelessly anti-Social. Perhaps, in his heart, Mr. Brock would hardly admit the absolute value of æsthetic rapture; he wants art to do something for life, and he loses patience with people who simply add to its confusion. Shelley, he thought, made a mess of his own life and of Harriet's, and, for all one knows, of Miss Hitchener's, and of a score of others; and his poetry you must read for its own sake or not at all. The poetry of Morris has value for people who have never known what it is to feel an æsthetic emotion, and his life was superbly useful to his fellow-men. The great State of the future will be glad of as many William Morrises as it can get.

But it is I who am being less than just now. From what I have said any one might infer that I had not read, or had not appreciated, that volume called "The Defence of Guenevere and Other Poems," in which are to be found things of pure beauty, "Summer Dawn," "In Prison," "The Wind," "The Haystack in the Floods"; any one might suppose that I did not know "Love is Enough." These are the poems which, with "Sigurd," give William Morris his place amongst the poets. Mr. Clutton Brock feels this surely enough, because he possesses, besides intellect, that other and rarer critical faculty, that spiritual tuning-fork by which a fine critic distinguishes between emotion and sentimentality, between rhetoric and rant. It is because Mr. Brock possesses this peculiar sensibility—part æsthetic, part ethical, and part intellectual, it seems—that he can be trusted to detect and dislike even the subtlest manifestations of that quality which most distinguishes Tennyson from Morris, Kipling from Walt Whitman, and the Bishop of London from the Vicar of Wakefield. That is why I suppose Mr. Brock to be one of our best critics.

If there were anything fundamentally nasty about Morris Mr. Brock would not be inclined to overrate him. Mr. Brock pardons no unpardonable horrors: there are none here to pardon. But he overrates, or rather overmarks, William Morris as a scrupulous but soft-hearted examiner might overmark a sympathetic pupil. He never gives marks when the answer is wrong, but he gives a great many when it is right: and he is a little blind to deficiencies. He does not make it clear that Morris, as an artist, was cursed with two of the three modern English vices, that he was provincial and amateurish. But he gives him full credit for not being goaded to futility by a sense of his own genius.

Morris was provincial as the Pre-Raphaelites and Tennyson and Carlyle were provincial, as Swinburne and Whistler were not; his mind could rarely escape from the place and age in which it was formed. He looked at art and life, and at the future even, from the point of view of an Englishman and a Victorian; and when he tries to change his position we feel the Victorian labouring, more or less unsuccessfully, to get out of himself. When I accuse him of being "amateurish" I do not use that vile word in contradistinction to "professional." In a sense all true artists must be amateurs; the professional view, the view that art is a hopeful and genteel way of earning one's living, is possible only to official portrait-painters and contractors for public monuments. When I say that Morris, like almost all our visual artists and too many of our modern writers, was amateurish, I mean that he was not serious enough about his art. He tended to regard art as a part of life instead of regarding life as a means to art. A long morning's work, an afternoon of fresh air, a quiet evening, and so to bed and fit next morning for another good spell of production; something of that sort, one fancies, was not unlike the ideal of William Morris. It is a craftsman's ideal; it is a good life for any one but an artist; and it would be a good attitude towards art if art were not something altogether different from work. Alas! it is the English attitude. I never look at those Saxon manuscripts in the British Museum but I say to myself: "And didn't they go out and have a game of cricket after hours and work all the harder next day for their wholesome exercise!"

But from the fatal curse Morris was free; no man of great ability was ever less conceited. You will not find in his work a trace of that tired pomposity which tells us that the great man is showing off, or of that empty pretentious singularity which betrays the vanity of the lonely British artist. Morris was never the self-conscious master calling on sun and moon to stand and watch him sign his name, neither was he the shy genius of the English hedgerows sheltering his little talent from contemporary infection and the chill winds of criticism.

Morris was neither a great artist nor a great thinker, but he was a great man, and that, I suspect, is the chief reason why Mr. Brock loves him, and why none of the better sort can help liking him. He had that magnanimity which makes people take instinctively the right side. His reasons might be wrong, but he was in the right. There are people in history, and Morris is one of them, about whom we feel that if they were alive they would sympathize with whatever were the best and most pressing aspirations of the age. Morris would, of course, be as firm to-day as ever against plutocracy, but one feels sure that he would take his stand with those who are trying to win for themselves some kind of moral and intellectual as well as economic freedom. One feels sure he would be of that forlorn hope of civilization that carries on a sporadic and ineffective war against officialism and militarism on the one hand, and puritanism and superstition on the other. One feels sure that, however little he might like new developments in art or thought, he would be against the people who tried to suppress them. One feels quite sure that he would never cease to believe that so long as society is imperfect it is the right and duty of individuals to experiment. The fact is, Morris was at once a practical craftsman and an idealist. In practical affairs and private prejudices he could be as truculent and wrong-headed as the rest of us; but he was always conscious of something much more important than practical affairs and private prejudices. He cared nothing for his own reputation and little for immediate success because he cared for something greater. For that he cared so much that he was able to forgive the quarrels and absurdities of the Hammersmith Socialists and to laugh even at his own vehemence.

FOOTNOTE:

[15] "William Morris." By A. Clutton Brock. (Williams and Norgate: Home University Library, 1s. net.)

PERSIAN MINIATURES[16]

Burlington Magazine May 1914

Very slowly it is becoming possible to construct a history of Persian painting. Until quite lately all attempts were frustrated by what is sure to frustrate the attempts of the first historians of any "school" or "slope," or, for that matter, of any subject whatever—a false point of departure. So long as it was supposed that Behzad was the first mature master of Persian painting, Persian art-historians were as inevitably out in their conjectures as were the people who used to believe that Raphael was what they would have called "the *fons et origo*" of European painting.

We are now acquainted, if not familiar, with Persian paintings of the thirteenth and early fourteenth centuries, with the Mongol and with a pre-Mongol school—for it seems imprudent to give the name Mongol to works that can be assigned to a date earlier than 1258 (the year of the eponymous establishment), especially as they differ profoundly from the recognized Mongol type. We know that the pre-Mongol school was the heir of a great decorative tradition; and we have good reasons for believing that this tradition was based on Sassanian, Sung, and Byzantine art. We are therefore more or less in the position of people who should be acquainted with the work of Cimabue, Giotto, and Duccio, though knowing very little of Byzantine art and its primitive developments in the West.

Of this early period—Mongol and pre-Mongol—we do not yet possess many examples; but the student who turns to the *Burlington Magazine* for July and August 1913 will see reproductions from a superb manuscript of the late thirteenth century, Mr. Pierpont Morgan's "Manafi-i-Heiwan," and any one who has the good fortune to know M. Claude Anet or M. Vignier can probably be put in the way of seeing some originals. He will discover in the work of this early period two distinct schools: one—of which the running ibexes in the "Manafi-i-Heiwan" is an example—obviously related to Sung; the other—of which the "Kalila and Dimna" miniatures[17] (dated 1236), and the elephants from the "Manafi-i-Heiwan" (1295 *circa*) may be taken as illustrations—reminding us rather of Sassanian art. Exquisite perfection of line is the dominant characteristic of the first school; in the second, we find a broader treatment, a more splendid disposition of masses, and a more monumental design than in any other known school of Persian painting. It is amongst the works of these thirteenth-century painters that we must look for the discovered masterpieces of Persian art.

In our present state of ignorance we may call this the great age. It is the familiar age of fine Rhages pottery; and to compare the beautiful drawing on the twelfth-and thirteenth-century pots with the miniatures of this period is to let a flood of light on to the study of both. Mr. Kevorkian has, or had, a wonderful painting from "The History of the Kalifs" by Tabari (about 1200), the figures of which might have walked straight out of a Rhages bowl into which they had walked some fifty years earlier direct from Western China. Yet, admirable as this thirteenth century is, I do not believe that it is in fact the supreme age of Persian painting. Certainly it is not the primitive age. This is an art that comes out of a long tradition. And just as we have already discovered pottery earlier than and surpassing that of the thirteenth century, so I hope and believe we shall yet see primitive Persian paintings superior to anything that the late pre-Mongol and Mongol period can show. For the present we can only say that the works of this period are not much inferior to the greatest that the genius of any race or age has created.

In 1335 begins what is known as the Timourid age—the age beloved above all others by discerning connoisseurs—and it is tempting to assign to this famous period the illustrations in a manuscript belonging to Mr. Herramaneck, now in the possession of Mr. Arthur Ruck, from which are drawn the paintings reproduced on Plate I. This temptation is strengthened by the fact that the manuscript is said to be dated 1398; yet it is a temptation to which I am unwilling to yield. Rather, I incline to think that these are the work of an early contemporary of Behzad, by whom they are not influenced, and that they belong, therefore, to that interesting period of transition which lies between the Timourids of the fifteenth and the Sefevaeans of the sixteenth century. If we turn to the *Burlington Magazine* for October 1912, we can compare our Plate I, a, with two paintings, one in M. Claude Anet's collection dating from the fourteenth century, the other from M. Meyer-Riefstahl's belonging to the fifteenth. All have Mongol affinities: but in M. Anet's picture, though the rather finicking and academic drawing of the tree shows that already under the early Timourids the full Persian style was developed, there are yet to be found traces of a monumental design that had almost disappeared by the end of the fifteenth century.

The work here illustrated is too "descriptive" and not sufficiently "monumental" to be assigned to the Timourid age, and so I give it to the late fifteenth century, to those delicious years when the old tradition, though weakened, had not been smothered under the scenic delicacies brought into fashion by Behzad. If the Timourid age is to be dubbed the Persian *quattrocento*, Mr. Ruck's man will pass muster as the counterpart of some artist older than Raphael, who worked independently of the young prodigy unaffected by his ultimately disastrous inventions.

From an album, also in the possession of Mr. Arthur Ruck, comes a drawing signed by Behzad and reproduced on Plate II, c. On the genuineness of the signature I cannot pretend to an opinion, but there seem to be no solid grounds for disputing it. The work itself is characteristic enough. It is accomplished and tasteful; it is also thin in quality and the forms are indifferently co-ordinated. It is, in fact, a very pretty piece of illustration; it is not a profoundly moving design. Compared with figure A on Plate I it is tight and unlovely: compared with the masterpieces of the thirteenth century it is not even what a picture by Raphael is to a picture by Giotto; if, historically, Behzad is the Raphael of Persia, æsthetically, he is a very inferior one.

It is in the post-Behzad art, their Sefevaean art of the sixteenth century, that the Persians have the advantage of us. The miniatures of this age were, until lately, reckoned by European collectors the masterpieces of Persian painting, and the decline of their reputation may be compared with that of those later *cinquecentiste* who stood so high in the taste of the eighteenth century. The descent, however, has been less sharp as the error was less glaring. After Behzad there is no such tumble as befell Italian art in the last days of the Renaissance. On the contrary, as my final illustrations (also drawn from Mr. Ruck's scrap-book) show, the Persian art of the sixteenth century maintained a very high level. The ladder picture (Plate III, D) is, I presume, by Sultan Mohamed. For my part I prefer it to the Behzad. It is less mechanical; and I find in it none of that weary pomposity, that gesture of the great man who knows his business too well, which so often displeases me in the master. Sultan Mohamed was, so the story goes, a pupil of Aga Mirek, who was a pupil of Behzad.

This charming Sultan Mohamed belongs to the middle of the sixteenth century, and its companion illustration (Plate III, E) may be placed some twenty years later. About this last, however, it would be easy and excusable to go wrong; for from the local colour and the head of the man who leads the horse it would seem to have been painted in India. We know that the album from which it comes was for many years in that country; yet I cannot believe that this picture is the product of any Indo-Persian school. It is too good: there persists too much of the great Timourid and Mongol tradition which, as the work of Sultan Mohamed shows, was still cherished by the Persian artists of the sixteenth century. That it is earlier than the seventeenth century and the reign of Shah Abbas is beyond dispute; it is untainted, or almost untainted, with that soft, slick, convictionless woolliness that was brought to perfection by Riza Abbassi, the court painter, and seems to have flattered so happily the taste of the Persian *grand monarque*. The figure of the kneeling princess comes nearer to the style of Mirek than to that of any other artist with whom I am acquainted; and, if I must hazard a guess, I will suggest that this is the work of some Persian pupil of Mirek who went to try his luck at the court of the Great Mogul.

With Shah Abbas and the seventeenth century Persian art becomes definitely and hopelessly second-rate. From the ruins emerge a variety of decadent schools of which two deserve mention. The academic school continued the Behzad tradition, and its hard but capable style did well enough for copying Persian old masters, European paintings by such artists as Bellini, and engravings by such artisans as Marcantonio—an amusing product of this last kind of activity (also from a book in Mr. Ruck's possession) will be reproduced later in the *Burlington Magazine*. At the same time there appeared a freer and softer style, examples of which, at first sight, sometimes remind one of a particularly good Conder. In India developed a number of schools, romantic, picturesque, and literal; of these, a queer sensual charm notwithstanding, it must be confessed that the two main characteristics are weakness of design and a sweetly sugary colour. But I am straying beyond any boundary that my illustrations could justify. I have been able to give excellent examples of the late middle period of Persian painting. In the two first we caught an echo of the great Timourid age and felt a premonition of the good Sefevaean: in the last we see how splendid Persian painting could be in its decline. I wish I could have reproduced examples to show how glorious was its youth and early manhood.

FOOTNOTES:

[16] To make the most of an article of this sort the reader ought, obviously, to have illustrations by him. For these, in the original even, I was obliged to refer to back numbers of the *Burlington Magazine*, and now I must refer also to the plates that accompanied this article when first it appeared.

[17] In the collections of M. Henraux and M. Claude Anet. Reproduced in the *Burlington Magazine*, October 1912.

COUNTERCHECK QUARRELSOME

New Statesman Mar. 1914

I hasten to accept Mr. Randall Davies's offer of friendship,[18] though I doubt whether much good can come of it if we are to go on arguing about æsthetics. We are too far apart. What Mr. Davies feels for a picture is something altogether different from what he feels for a carpet, whereas the emotion I feel for a carpet is of exactly the same kind as the emotion I feel for a picture, a statue, a cathedral, or a pot. Also, my whole system of æsthetics is based on this psychological fact, so that it would, perhaps, have been wiser in Mr. Davies to have stated the difference between us and let it go at that.

If some one were to find fault with the *New Statesman* on account of the flimsiness and inadequacy of the arguments it adduces in favour of private ownership of railways, the editor, being a polite man, would reply, I suppose, that his critic had misunderstood the policy of the paper: he would not feel that his arguments had received any very damaging blow. In my first chapter I made it clear—my publishers accused me of becoming repetitious about it—that what I wanted to discover was a quality common and peculiar to all those objects I called works of art; I explained that by "works of art" I meant objects that provoked in me a peculiar emotion, called æsthetic; and I repeated over and over again that amongst these objects were pictures, pots, textiles, statues, buildings, etc. Mr. Davies's sharp eyes have enabled him to perceive either that my hypothesis—that "significant form" is the essential quality in a work of art—leads to the inclusion of Persian carpets amongst works of art, or that the hypothesis that representation is the essence of art excludes them: I am not sure which. Anyway, this much is certain, either both pictures and carpets can be works of art or they cannot. I set out from the hypothesis that pictures and carpets, or rather some pictures and some carpets, are works of art; and therefore I am less inclined to feel crushed by Mr. Davies's discovery that my premises follow from my conclusions than to inquire why Mr. Davies does not consider carpets and pots and buildings works of art, or, if, after all, he does consider them works of art, to what class he relegates pictures and statues. My object is to discover some quality common and peculiar to all works of art. Such a quality there must be unless when we use the term "works of art" we gibber. Does Mr. Davies assert that only pictures and statues can be works of art? Or are we to assume that he gibbers?

Even if I cannot argue profitably with my new friend I may be able to give him a useful hint. For though, as he wittily observes, he is still much older than I am, it is conceivable that I enjoy a wider æsthetic experience.

> "To look for the same qualities in a carpet and a picture would be equally absurd, seeing that one is intended to hang on the wall and the other to be laid on the floor. If any one doubts this, let him frame his carpets and put his canvases over the parquet."

To hang on the wall was, of course, precisely the purpose for which many of the finest Oriental carpets were intended; but disdaining all considerations, no matter how relevant, that seem to set a premium on scholarship, I will gladly put my friend and his readers in the way of carrying out this interesting experiment. They need not jeopardize the drawing-room furniture. Not far from the house in which Mr. Davies lives stands a building so large and so silly that it can scarcely have escaped his admiration. It is the Victoria and Albert Museum; and any one who cares to step inside can see a fair collection of Oriental carpets hanging picture-wise against the wall—hanging in frames too. I shall be very much surprised if the more sensitive of those who trouble to pay them a visit do not feel that these carpets are as æsthetically satisfactory on the wall as they would be on the floor, and I shall be amazed if they do not feel also that they are as definitely works of art as the objects that adorn the walls of the Tate Gallery.

My purpose is to discover the quality common and peculiar to works of art. I have suggested that this quality is what I call Significant Form—i.e. combinations of lines and colours that are in themselves moving. A good many people besides Mr. Davies have blamed me for giving the name Significant Form to just that form which seems to signify nothing. I adopted the term with hesitation, and I shall sacrifice it without pain if something better can be found to take its place. All the same, I did try to explain what I meant by it. I speak of Significant Form in contradistinction to Insignificant Beauty—the beauty of gems or of a butterfly's wing, the beauty that pleases, but does not seem to provoke that peculiar thrill that we call an æsthetic emotion. I suggested very cautiously that the explanation of this difference might lie in the fact that the forms created by an artist express, or in some way transmit, an emotion felt by their creator, whereas the forms of nature, so far as most of us are concerned, do not seem to hand on anything so definite. But about this part of my theory I was, and still am, extremely diffident, and I mention it here only in the hope of justifying what has seemed to many sensible people a silly name.

At the beginning of my book I was at some pains to explain why I held that all systems of æsthetics must be based on personal experience. I said that my purpose was to discover some quality common and peculiar to all works that moved me æsthetically, and I invited those whose experience did not tally with mine—and whose experience does tally exactly with that of any one else?—to discover some other quality common and peculiar to all the objects that so moved them. I said that in elaborating a theory of æsthetics an author must depend entirely on his own experience, and in my book I depended entirely on mine. There are people to whom a simple statement of this sort comes as a pressing invitation to score cheaply:—So now we know what art is, it is whatever you are pleased to honour with your approval. "But why should Mr. Bell suppose that the forms that move him are the only ones proper to move others?" says Mr. Davies.

> "Again, it is as foolish for Mr. Bell, or any other individual, to say, as he does say, that Frith's *Paddington Station* is not a work of art as it would be for me to say that rhubarb tart—which I detest—is not food. If I were the only person in the world who ate anything, then, I admit, I should be right in saying that it was not food—for it would not be, because I should never eat it. And if Mr. Bell were the only spectator of works of art on earth, he would have a perfect right to say that *Paddington Station* was not a work of art. But as he is not the only person on earth—if he will forgive me for mentioning the fact—he has no right to say that it is not a work of art."

If this were anything more respectable than one of those pieces of grave but delicate sarcasm for which I am told Mr. Davies is famous, it would be perilous doctrine in the mouth of a professional art critic. We have no right to say that something is not a work of art so long as other people say that it is. The poor fellow who has gone through with a picture to the very end and has got it hung will always, I suspect, consider it a work of art; and I hope that some of his friends will have the humanity to back him up. Therefore ... well, we must be catholic. But Mr. Randall Davies, who deals out, week after week, column after column of æsthetic judgments, may surely be invited by his readers to disclose the criteria by which he distinguishes between works of art and rubbish. If a work of art be that which any one judges to be a work of art, we may as well consult the first policeman we meet instead of going for an opinion to a paid expert.

If Mr. Davies had understood the very simple language in which I stated my position, he would have realized that when I say that *Paddington Station* is not a work of art I mean that *Paddington Station* does not provoke in me an æsthetic emotion, and that I believe we can have no reason for thinking a thing to be a work of art except that we feel it to be one. *Paddington Station* did not move me; therefore I had no reason for judging it a work of art, but, of course, I may have looked at the picture stupidly and remained insensitive to the real significance of its forms. If Mr. Davies had understood the very simple language in which I stated my position, he would have realized that, far from making a claim to infallibility in æsthetic judgments, I insisted on the fact that we might all disagree about particular works of art and yet agree about æsthetics. But if Mr. Davies had been able to catch the general drift of my book, he would have understood that whether *Paddington Station* moves me or whether it leaves me cold is a matter of secondary importance. The point of first importance is whether a person who is moved in the same sort of way by *Paddington Station* and a Sung bowl and Sta. Sophia and a Persian carpet can find any quality common and peculiar to all save that which I have called Significant Form.

That is the problem. It is not quite so simple as I have had to make it appear. Some day I hope to answer the pertinent questions raised by Mr. Roger Fry and other critics. In my book I have examined my own experience in the hope of inducing my readers to examine theirs. What do they say? Are they really talking nonsense when they speak of "works of art," including under that head pictures, pots, buildings, textiles, etc.? If they are not, what characteristic distinguishes the species? Do they not feel as much emotion for a picture of a round of beef as for a picture of the Crucifixion, and do they feel less for a Sassanian textile? If what they had taken for a jug turns out to be a paper-weight; if, as sometimes happens in a battered fresco, what was said to be the Heavenly host is proved to be a pack of licentious Florentines, do they really have to readjust their æsthetic attitude? If people who are capable of feeling and of analysing their feelings will give me honest answers to these questions, I shall be even more grateful to them than I am to Mr. Davies for his facetious advertisement of my book.

FOOTNOTE:

[18] I wonder what Mr. Davies really said. Any one who cares to know has only to consult the *New Statesman* for March 7 or 14, 1914. I have not a copy by me. It looks as though there had been a pretty firm offer of some sort: it came to nothing, alas!

PICTURE SHOWS

I

THE LONDON SALON

Athenæum July 1912

There are many reasons for approving of the London Salon. For one thing it is the only place in England where pictures are hung without any selection being made. The fate of the Salon d'Automne, formerly the most interesting exhibition in Europe, could be cited to discredit the jury system, were it not that the system had discredited itself even more effectually in this country by making it appear that British art had ceased to exist. No matter how good the intentions of a jury may be, inevitably it comes to be dominated by a clique of painters who imagine that they are setting a high standard by rejecting all pictures sufficiently unlike their own. In France, therefore, "Les Indépendants" have become the representatives of contemporary art, while English people who hope to discover something vital at home must betake themselves to the Albert Hall.

But there is more than this to be said for the London Salon: its standard of painting is far higher than that of the Royal Academy or of the New English Art Club. For this we have chiefly to thank Mr. Walter Sickert and his pupils. They set the tone. It is extraordinary that any master should have led so many pupils so far along the road to art. All have been taken to that point where work ceases to appear utterly negligible. All have been made to search life for realities, and not for pictures. They have been taught to simplify and to select; and they have been taught not to select the obvious, the romantic, and the pretty. They have not been taught, however, to discover and express the profoundly significant, for that cannot be taught. Even Mr. Sickert cannot turn sincere and intelligent painters into artists.

Entering the arena, the visitor will probably turn first to the large picture by Mr. Wyndham Lewis. To appreciate this, he should take the lift to the gallery, whence, having shed all irrelevant prejudices in favour of representation, he will be able to contemplate it as a piece of pure design. He will be able to judge it as he would judge music—that is to say, as pure, formal expression. So judging, he cannot fail to be impressed by the solidity of the composition, to which the colour is not an added charm, but of which it is an integral part; he will feel that the picture holds together as a unity in the way that a good sonata holds, in a way that nothing else does in this exhibition; also he will feel a certain dissatisfaction which may cause him to inquire whether Mr. Lewis has altogether succeeded in expressing himself. We believe that he has not. There is a laboriousness about this work which seems to represent the artist's unsuccessful struggle to realize in paint his mental conception; and it is for this reason that we admire it rather as a promise of something great than as an achievement.

The other striking thing in the arena is Mr. Epstein's statue. Approached from behind, as the present writer approached it, this has very much the air of an important work of art; and that it well may be. Closer examination, however, raises some doubts. Is it, perhaps, only the imitation of one? Mr. Epstein is a baffling artist. His skill and scholarship are amazing, and he seems to have convictions; but what are they? Has he merely a brilliant gift for description, helped out and sophisticated by a subtle taste? Or has he a queer entangled sense of the significance of form. Is he a plastic artist or an extraordinarily gifted statuary? Even if this work be an imitation, how admirable a one is it! That Mr. Epstein should combine with the taste and intelligence to perceive the beauty of Mexican sculpture the skill and science to reproduce its fine qualities is surely something to note and admire. There is enough in this figure, imitative though it be, to secure for its author pre-eminence amongst living British sculptors.[19]

A third work in this part of the hall has attracted some attention. It is a picture of the coronation of George V. by one Fernand Piret, a French aviator—so the story goes—who never before dabbled in terrene arts. It may be so. In any case he has contrived a mordant comment on that memorable and mystic ceremony.

Upstairs, the best things are two charming pictures by Mr. S. F. Gore. It is a joy to watch the progress of this good artist. The patient and unpretentious labour of his experimental years is being handsomely rewarded. Mr. Gore is finding himself; we never doubted that he was well worth finding. Mr. Gilman, too, is steadily becoming more interesting; but Mr. Ginner has, as yet, hardly fulfilled the promise of his early work. The delicate sensibility and fine scholarship which M. Lucien Pissarro chooses to conceal beneath a presentment of almost exaggerated modesty will escape no one whose eyes have not been blinded by the flush of fashionable vulgarity, of which, happily, there is very little here. The London Salon is no place for those who are, or who hope to become, portrait-makers at "a thousand" a head.

All the creditable work to be found in this exhibition is not to be mentioned in one article. The pictures by Miss Helen Saunders, painted surely under the influence of Mr. Etchells; *The Omnibus*, by Mr. Adeney; the works of Mrs. Louise Pichard, Mr. Malcolm Drummond, Mr. J. B. Yeats, and Mr. W. B. C. Burnet; that rather pretentious piece, *Les Deux Amies*, by Madame Renée Finch; and *The Cot*, a charming little picture by Mrs. Ogilvie—all deserve more attention than any overworked critic is likely to give them. They are, for the most part, accomplished paintings that provoke no doubts and no outrageous hopes.

FOOTNOTE:

[19] 1917: A friendly critic reading this paragraph suggests that it might stand fairly as a description of Meštrović. I cannot agree. Epstein is in every respect superior to the Serbian sculptor, in whose work there can be no question of anything but *pastiche*. It has been said that it expresses the soul of Serbia. I know nothing of that. What I do know, what every one familiar with modern art knows, is that it expresses nothing but what can be learnt by any clever student in the schools of Vienna, Munich, and Paris.

II

ENGLISH POST-IMPRESSIONISTS

Nation Oct. 1913

It is said that Cézanne was in the habit of describing himself as a pupil of Camille Pissarro. The belief is popular, and may be well founded; at any rate, it has emboldened Mr. Rutter to overstock his "Post-Impressionist and Futurist Exhibition" with unimportant works by this distinguished Impressionist. Surely a couple of examples would have sufficed to illustrate the latest, and best, theory of æsthetics. For that is the service performed on this occasion by the works of Pissarro. They mark that difference in purpose between three schools, an understanding of which will enable the intelligent student to pick his way across the depths and shallows of contemporary art.

The romantic artists of the early nineteenth century used form and colour to describe situations and comment on life. There are no examples of their work in this exhibition; but, as we shall see, the Futurists are unconsciously harking back to their theories. The Impressionists, in rebellion, used form and colour to register their visual impressions; they belong to the age of science and state facts without comment. But every romantic or impressionist painter who happened to be an artist also used form and colour as means of expressing and provoking pure æsthetic emotion. It was not his fault if he flew in the face of party principles; he was an artist and he could not help it. Cézanne was not only a very great artist; he was what is almost as rare, a thoughtful one. So, in his later periods, he came to use form and colour solely as means of expressing and provoking those extraordinary emotions that arise from the contemplation of real or imagined form. His theory quarrels with no vital school of art that has ever existed. He merely sifted the grain from the chaff, the relevant from the irrelevant.

The Lake, by Cézanne, is therefore the most important æsthetic document in this exhibition besides being the best picture. Cézanne set modern art on the right road. The revolutionary doctrine he bequeathed to Post-Impressionism is a truth as old as the Neolithic Age—the truth that forms and colours are of themselves significant. The Italian Futurists are at the opposite pole to Post-Impressionists because they treat form and colour as vehicles for the transmission of facts and ideas. *Polka* and *Valse* by Severini are, in intention, as descriptive as *The Doctor* by Sir Luke Fildes; only they are meant to describe states of mind, whereas *The Doctor* purports to describe a situation. Whether, in fact, they succeed in describing anything, and, if so, whether what they describe is of much consequence, are questions for the psychologist. The critic of art has only to note that the forms and colours are in themselves insignificant and in their relations commonplace; they are also those much affected of late by the more adventurous students at the École des Beaux-Arts.

Futurism is a negligible accident: the discoveries of Cézanne are safe in the hands of the French masters, with whose names the catalogue bristles—Gauguin, Van Gogh, Matisse, Picasso, Marchand, Derain, Marquet, Friesz, Herbin, l'Hote. Unluckily, the big artists are, for the most part, meagrely represented by rather unimportant works, of which, by the way, a good many are already familiar to picture-goers. I think I never met so many old faces in a modern exhibition. And though I shall never complain of encountering a Matisse or a Marchand, though it be for the third time in eighteen months, to be vexed by some mediocre remnant from the summer exhibitions strikes me as an unnecessarily sharp tax on the patience.

I do not grumble at the reappearance of Wyndham Lewis's *Kermesse*, which has been altered and greatly improved since its last appearance at the London Salon. Lewis promises to become that rare thing, a real academic artist. He is academic in the good sense of the word—that is to say, he uses a formula of which he is the master and not the slave. He uses it as a means to vast organizations of form, designed, I imagine, to have something of the austere and impressive unity of great architecture. He succeeds to a surprising degree. The enemy that dogs him in all his works is an excessive taste for life. He is inclined to modify his forms in the interest of drama and psychology, to the detriment of pure design. At times his simplifications and rhythms seem to be determined by a literary rather than a plastic conception. Probably this is not the kind of criticism which by now Wyndham Lewis must have learnt to disregard. He is more accustomed, I suspect, to hearing his work called "mechanical" and "lifeless," and, in a sense, it is both. That is the price an artist must pay who sets himself to achieve the end that Lewis has in view. He who is working by formula towards the realization of a minutely definite intellectual plan must be willing, on occasions, to sacrifice the really valuable qualities of sensibility and handwriting as well as the adventitious charms that spring from happy flukes. Besides, I am not sure that Lewis has been blest with uncommon sensibility.

The peculiar merits of *Kermesse* will become obvious to any one who, after contemplating that picture, turns sharp round and glances at the big canvas by Delaunay. Delaunay, according to Mr. Rutter, is "the protagonist" of what is known in Paris as "Orféism"; his picture, *The Cardiff Football Team*, is what used to be known in Paris as *très artiste*. It is well made, but it is not made to wear. It is not what Cézanne would have called "quelque chose de solide et de durable comme l'art des musées." It is a brighter, gayer, more attractive thing than *Kermesse*, but in construction it is less subtle and less solid: by comparison, it looks like a poster, and a poster, I believe, is what it is.

It would be tedious to write at length about the French masters, considering how much has been written during the last twelve months in praise or blame of finer and more characteristic examples of their art. More profitably they may be used as a peg on which to hang a short sermon to their English imitators. Amongst these I do not reckon the painters of the Camden Town group, of whose work there is plenty in this exhibition. Walter Sickert, the chief of that school, was in possession of a style and a reputation when Picasso was still making figures on a slate. Spencer Gore has taken from the new movement just so much as was suited to his temperament, and, without submitting his personal gift to any formula, has added immensely to the significance and charm of his work. The majority, however, remain essentially what they have always been—realistic impressionists. They have been very conscientiously twisting their hurdy-gurdies while Rome was a-burning.

But, as this exhibition shows, there is a school of English Post-Impressionists. It is not completely represented here; indeed, the gaps are as conspicuous as they are unfortunate. Here we have only a heterogeneous collection of young painters, diverse in talent and temper, all of whom have this in common, that they have swallowed, more or less whole, the formulas which French masters invented and which French masters are now developing and modifying. Confronted by the elaborate surprises of these rank-and-file men, the patriotic critic, supposing such an anomaly to exist, will have to admit that English painting remains where it has generally been—in a by-street. It is well to admit this in time; for I can almost hear those queer people who can appreciate what is vital in every age but their own, squealing triumphantly—"We told you so." Yes; it is true. English Post-Impressionism is becoming academic: but Post-Impressionism is not; in France the movement is as vital as ever.

Too many of the English Post-Impressionists are coming to regard certain simplifications, schematizations, and tricks of drawing, not as means of expression and creation, but as ends in themselves, not as instruments, but as party favours. The French masters are being treated by their English disciples as Michael Angelo and Titian were treated by the minor men of the seventeenth century. Their mannerisms are the revolutionary's stock-in-trade. One is constantly confronted at the Doré Gallery by a form or a colour that is doing no æsthetic work at all; it is too busy making a profession of faith; it is shouting, "I am advanced—I am advanced." I have no quarrel with advanced ideas or revolutionary propaganda; I like them very well in their place, which I conceive to be a tub in the park. But no man can be at once a protestant and an artist. The painter's job is to create significant form, and not to bother about whether it will please people or shock them. Ugliness is just as irrelevant as prettiness, and the painter who goes out of his way to be ugly is being as inartistic and silly as the man who makes his angels simper. That is what is the matter with Hamilton's portrait in the big room—to take an instance at random. Hamilton has plenty of talent, and this picture is well enough, pleasant in colour and tastefully planned; but his talent would be seen to greater advantage if it did not strut in borrowed and inappropriate plumes. The simplifications and distortion of the head perform, so far as I can see, no æsthetic function whatever; they are not essential to the design, and are at odds with the general rhythm of the picture. Had the painter scribbled across his canvas, "To hell with everything," it seems to me he would have done what he wanted to do, and done it better.

What gives even minor Frenchmen an advantage over the English is artistic courage. They will be themselves at all costs, even at the risk of pleasing old ladies from the country, or passing unnoticed. Asselin goes farther than Nevinson with less ability. Yet Nevinson bears the Briton's burden more lightly than his fellows; probably because he is cleverer than most of them. He is clever enough to pick up some one else's style with fatal ease; is he not clever enough to diagnose the malady and discover a cure? If I were older, I would advise Nevinson and the more intelligent of this company to shut themselves up for six months, and paint pictures that no one was ever going to see. They might catch themselves doing something more personal if less astonishing than what they are showing at the Doré Galleries. Artistic courage, that is what is wanted—courage to create the forms that express oneself instead of imitating those that express the people for whom one would gladly be mistaken.

III

AN EXPENSIVE "MASTERPIECE"

New Statesman July 1914

Because we all know stories of first-rate works of art having been offered at ridiculously low prices to English galleries and museums and refused by them on the ground that there was no money even for the purchase of what was very good and very cheap, we are surprised and even excited when we hear that a big price (some say as much as £5000) has been paid for a Chinese pottery figure. And those of us who have the fortune to belong to the privileged, and therefore well-behaved, sex hurry off to see what Mr. Hobson describes in the May number of the *Burlington Magazine* as "a new Chinese masterpiece in the British Museum."

Mr. Hobson is a sound archæologist; consequently it is impossible to read his careful and admirably frank article without surmising that he himself feels some qualms of suspicion about the date, if not the beauty, of his treasure. For us the first question to be asked is: "Is this a fine work of art?" For Mr. Hobson I suppose the first care was to decide whether or no the thing was T'ang. His is the sound, the scientific, the archæological method; and I feel sure he followed it because it is the archæological method, and because, had he followed the unscientific, æsthetic method, and considered first the style and artistic worth of this figure, he would have found that in answering our question he had answered his own or made the asking of it superfluous. Had Mr. Hobson been as sensitive as he is sound, we may be sure that he would have seen this so-called T'ang Lohan in America or farther before ever he advised the British Museum to bid a shilling for it.

The "new Chinese masterpiece in the British Museum" is a common, pretentious thing, and that, if I must play the archæologist, is a fair reason for suspecting that it is not the product of a great age—and T'ang art still seems great even after we have seen something of its greater predecessors, Wei, Liang, Sui. This figure, though larger than life-size, is nowise monumental; on the contrary, it is patently a *bibelot agrandi*, reminding one oddly in this respect of Benvenuto Cellini's *Perseus*. It is something that has been conceived on a small scale and carried out on a large. This fact alone, had it been noted, as it must have been by any one who looked at the figure æsthetically, would have suggested that this was a product, not of the T'ang dynasty—an age of monumental sculpture—but of the Ming dynasty—the great age of choice chinoiseries and archaistic experiments.

This theory—that the figure is Ming—technical evidence supports at least as strongly as it supports the T'ang attribution. Technique apart, artistic consideration makes it clear that if the work is not T'ang it must be as late as Ming. That this should be so may at first seem strange to those who remember that the T'ang dynasty flourished between A.D. 618 and 906, and the Ming between 1368 and 1643. Yet, in fact, it is far easier to confuse T'ang with Ming than to confuse a work of the intermediate Sung period (960-1279) with either. The mystery is not profound. Throughout the T'ang and Sung periods Chinese art was thoroughly alive; both T'ang and Sung are vital and original styles. T'ang art expresses the inspiration of one age, Sung of another; Sung follows and differs from T'ang as *quattrocento* follows and differs from Giottesque: they are different and characteristic modes of a continuous stream of inspiration. But the Sung dynasty and the Chinese inspiration collapsed within a hundred years or less of each other, and for suggestion and direction the Ming artists looked, not so much into their own hearts as to the past, and especially to the golden days of T'ang. History is deaf to the doctrine of progressive evolution, and, if we would understand the history of art, we must learn to think in styles rather than in years; also we must become accustomed to remote derivations. It is possible to confound Renaissance work of the sixteenth century with Roman of the second; it is impossible to confuse either with their neighbours, Gothic and Byzantine. Similarly, it would be intolerable to mistake Ming for Sung, but excusable to mistake it for T'ang, and that, I believe, is just what Mr. Hobson has done.

But, to be frank, I care very little when or where this figure was made; what I care about is its æsthetic insignificance. Look at the modelling of the hands: they are as insensitive and convictionless as lumps of bread. Look at the tight, cheap realism of the head; the accents violent without being impressive, the choice of relief common. The chest is the best part of the thing, and that strikes me as being traditional rather than felt. The view of the figure in profile is less unsatisfactory than the view from in front: but look at those hands!

If this thing impresses any one, it must impress him by its dramatic and not by its plastic qualities; and that is not the way in which a fine T'ang figure impresses us. Here the design is petty and the forms, in themselves, flaccid and poor; but the tight, realistic face is made to gaze most melodramatically into eternity. It is melodrama, I fancy, that has taken the town by storm. Compare this overgrown knick-knack with some really fine T'ang piece or, better still, with one of those Wei figures which the Museum had lately the chance of acquiring at a very moderate price, and you will feel the difference between form that impresses by sheer æsthetic rightness and form that reminds you of the late Sir Henry Irving. With all its elaborate quietness, this deep-contemplative Lohan is just a piece of rhetoric: put it beside something first-rate and you will know what to think of it as surely as you know what to think of

I have spread its folds o'er the dying, adrift in a hopeless sea;

I have hurled it swift on the slaver, and seen the slave set free,

when you put that beside

He all their ammunition

And feats of war defeats

With plain heroic magnitude of mind....

Why is it always in purchases of this sort the nation sinks the best part of its miserable art fund? Well, in this case I think it is possible to follow the workings of official taste. Officials know as well as the rest of us that T'ang art is well thought of, and that without some important example of it no Oriental collection is deemed complete. But T'ang art, as a rule, is neither literary nor pretty nor at all the sort of thing the collecting class cares for. What this class really likes is the art of the eighteenth century and the art of the high Renaissance. Miraculously comes to light an important figure labelled T'ang yet rich in the dear, familiar qualities of Renaissance sculpture. As usual, the officials have got it both ways. Surely Providence had a hand in this, unless it was the dealers.

IV

MARCHAND

Preface. Carfax Exhibition, June 1915

Of the younger French artists Marchand seems to me the most interesting. By "the younger" I mean those who, though they descend from Cézanne, have been influenced, directly or indirectly, by Matisse or Picasso or both. These form a just distinguishable group sandwiched between the quasi-impressionists—Bonnard, Manguin, Vuillard—and the Cubists. To be precise, it is of a battered sandwich that they are the core; the jam oozes through on either side. It always does. That is why scholars and historians have a hard time of it.

I dare say Marchand would deny that he had been influenced by any one; for some strange reason artists like to suppose that, unlike all other living things, they are unaffected by their environment. The matter is of no consequence, but with the best will in the world I should find it hard to believe that the *Femme couchée devant un paysage* (No. 5) would have been just what it is if Gauguin had never existed, or that the scheme of the beautiful *Portrait de femme* (No. 4) owes nothing to Picasso. And isn't it pretty clear that Marchand would have painted in an altogether different style if Cézanne had never existed?

Believing, as I do, in the influence of one artist on another, I regard this exhibition as a piece of rare good fortune for British art. Marchand is eminent in just those qualities that we most lack. Above all things he is a painter. I am curious to hear what Mr. Sickert has got to say about his pictures; and I shall be disappointed if they do not wring from him what used to be the highest encomium on the lips of his old friend Degas—*C'est de la peinture!*

No living painter is more purely concerned with the creation of form, with the emotional significance of shapes and colours, than Marchand. To him, evidently, the function of a painter is to paint; the discussion of such interesting matters as Love, Life, Death, and "The grand for ever," he leaves to the literary gentlemen. He has nothing to say about Man's place in the Universe, or even in Camden Town; it is in combinations of lines and colours that he deals, and, as you may see, he has already produced some of extraordinary subtlety and significance. Before such a picture as No. 7 or No. 12 the most inveterate psychologist, should he happen to possess a grain of sensibility, must be dumb; unless he murmur respectfully the name of Chardin.

Marchand is neither a doctrinaire nor a timid Conservative. He is familiar with the work of Cézanne, Matisse, Picasso, and the whole Cubist school; and if by simplification, distortion, or what men of science would call "flat absurdity," he can in any way improve his composition, he does not hesitate to simplify, distort, or fly in the face of facts. He wants to create significant form, and all means to that end he finds good. But he is no doctrinaire. He never distorts or makes his pictures look queer on principle. He cares nothing for being in the fashion, neither does he eschew a novel eccentricity lest the nicest people should say that he is going a little too far. His work is uncompromisingly sincere. He neither protests against tradition nor respects it. He is an artist.

I shall not be surprised to hear that some critics consider Marchand dry and intellectual. Certainly he is not lyrical or charming. No picture by him has the ravishing loveliness of a Renoir or the delicious handling of a Duncan Grant. I suspect he paints all his big things in the studio. He makes sketches; and I shall be glad to hear what any one competently acquainted with the drawings of the old masters has to say about No. 39. But when he gets to work on his canvas I do not suppose he thinks of anything beyond the complete realization of a definite and perfectly elaborated scheme. There are no happy accidents or lucky flukes in his painting. It is as stark and solid as the work of Ingres or Mantegna. Some people call that sort of thing dry and intellectual; others call it masterly.

If English amateurs take kindly to these pictures they will do themselves great honour. They will prove that they can distinguish between the easy juxtaposition of pretty patches of colour and the profound and sensitive research of a true colourist; they will prove that they can distinguish between obvious relations and subtle harmonies; they will prove that they can recognize that quality which is common to works of art of all schools and ages, and that, when they see it, they like it. And those unlucky people who cannot, even in the presence of a work of art, forget for a moment all about politics and philanthropy, may like to remember that Marchand, too, has been unlucky. After great hardships he had just won his way to a position of some security when war broke out. He has lately been called up, not, I think, for active, but for some sort of military service. His pay, I believe, is one sou a day, and what happens to those who depend on him one does not care to imagine.

Marchand was born at Paris in 1883. His work is not unknown in England. Four of his pictures were shown at the Grafton Galleries in 1912; and not long ago I saw an exquisite little "still life" by him—No. 12 in this

Exhibition, unless I mistake—at the New English Art Club. I wonder how it got there.

———————————————

V

THE MANSARD GALLERY[20]

Nov. 1917

The collection of modern pictures made by Mr. Fry, and shown, first in Birmingham and then at the Mansard Gallery, is the most important we have seen in London since the beginning of the war—since the Grosvenor House show in the summer of 1914, to be exact. That the best exhibition we have seen for so long should be held in the best gallery is a bit of good luck which, in these unlucky days, seems extraordinary; but what seems miraculous almost is that Messrs. Heal and Sons seem positively to prefer good pictures to bad. I would, therefore, advise any one who thinks my advice worth having to keep an eye on the Mansard Gallery.

In this exhibition the best of the younger English artists—I am sorry there is nothing by Stanley Spenser, Wyndham Lewis, Bomberg or Roberts—are confronted by a handful of their French contemporaries. They are not confronted by the best of them: Mr. Fry has hung nothing by Matisse, Bonnard or Picasso, for instance, though, had he pleased, he could have shown a couple of pictures by the last-named, at any rate. He chose well, I dare say; but it is mere justice to admit that the only two French artists fairly represented are Marchand and de Vlaminck. For the rest, the single picture by l'Hote is a characteristic work of that engaging but not very formidable painter; the two small pictures by Friesz, good as they are, hardly rank among his masterpieces; there is in London at least one other work by Gris, and that, to my thinking, a better; while the Derain is by no means worthy of that eminent artist.

I wish we could have been shown three or four capital works by Derain, because there is no man in the modern movement more readily appreciated by people who care for painting, but boggle at the unfamiliar. I remember finding myself once in Kahnweiler's shop on the Boulevards with an extremely intelligent official from South Kensington, and I remember his admitting with excellent candour that, though the Picassos still puzzled him, he was a thorough convert to Derain. Naturally: how should a man of taste and erudition not appreciate the exquisite scholarship of an artist who can use the masters of painting as a very fine man of letters—Charles Lamb, for instance—uses the masters of literature? For Derain is one who has gone to the root of the matter and can remind you of the Siennese school or have a joke with Pinturicchio by a subtler method than quotation.

When such a one bases his art on Cézanne and the *douanier* Rousseau, treating them quite simply as masters, an intelligent spectator is bound to unlock his most finished prejudices and take another look at them.

Marchand and de Vlaminck dominate one end of the gallery. There are three pictures by each, they are admirably hung, and the effect produced by this pool of distinguished and beautifully ordered colour is marvellous. One is brought to a stand by that indescribable sense that has come to most of us on entering for the first time some well-arranged room in an important continental gallery—a sense of being in the presence of great art. Closer examination, without destroying the unity of effect, proves these two men to be about as different as two very good artists of the same school and country can be. On Marchand I said my say two years ago when I wrote a preface for his show at Carfax: he is pre-eminently solid and architectural, and obviously he is highly sensitive—by which I mean that his reactions to what he sees are intense and peculiar. But these reactions, one fancies, he likes to take home, meditate, criticize, and reduce finally to a rigorously definite conception. And this conception he has the power to translate into a beautifully logical and harmonious form. Power he seems never to lack: it would be almost impossible to paint better. I do not know which of Marchand's three pictures is the best; but whichever it be, it is the best picture in the gallery.

With de Vlaminck it is from a word to a blow, from a thrilling emotion to a finished picture. If Marchand is like a minor Milton—the comparison is not one to be pressed—de Vlaminck is like Keats. He is the most lyrical of the younger Frenchmen; the flash and sparkle of his pictures is the wonderfully close expression of a tremblingly delighted sensibility. Yet there is nothing sketchy about them. Consider his landscape (No. 65), and you will be astonished to find what a solid, self-supporting design these delicately graded tones and lightly brushed forms compose.

Only one Englishman holds his own with the French painters, and he, of course, is Duncan Grant. The challenge to another very interesting young Englishman is, however, more marked since the de Vlaminck of which I have just spoken has as its rival on the wall, at right angles to it, *The Mill* (No. 32), by Mark Gertler. The comparison made, what first strikes one is that the Gertler, for all its assertion of strength and its emphatic, heavy accents, looks flimsy beside its lightly brushed and airy neighbour. But *The Mill* is not the piece by which Gertler should be judged; let us look rather at his large and elaborate *Swing Boats*. I have seen better Gertlers than this; the insistent repetition of not very interesting forms makes it come perilously near what Mr. Fry calls in his preface "merely ornamental pattern-making," but it is a picture that enables one to see pretty clearly the strength and weakness of this remarkable person.

With a greater artistic gift, Mark Gertler's conviction and conscience would suffice to make him a painter of the first magnitude. Unfortunately, his artistic gift, one inclines to suppose, is precisely that irreducible minimum without which an artist cannot exist. That is his weakness. His strength is that he exploits that minimum uncompromisingly to its utmost possibility. Gertler is one who will never say an idle word in paint, no matter how charming or interesting or amusing it might be. In his pictures you will look in vain for a single brush-stroke that does not serve his single purpose; he admits no adventitious dainties, there is nothing to quote. Happy touches are not in his way. Should he find some part of his picture empty he will not fill it with nicely balancing daisies, clouds, or bric-à-brac; he will begin it again. To him it will seem either that he has failed to conceive his work as a whole or that he has failed to realize his conception. Similarly, you will not easily discover a favourite passage; for if he felt that he had succeeded beyond expectation in one passage, that some note was sharper and truer than the rest, he would set himself to key the rest to that note. In art, such a process means incredible labour and agony; Gertler sweats blood and shows it. He labours terribly, and his pictures are terribly laboured. He is not artist enough to paint as a bird sings; he paints as a desperate soldier might dig himself in.

What he has to express is not, it must be confessed, of the highest quality, because his reactions are limited and rather undistinguished. He has only two or three notes, and they are neither rich nor rare. For an artist he is unimaginative, and often in their blank simplicity his conceptions are all but commonplace. In actual expression, too, though a first-rate craftsman who paints admirably, he lacks sensibility. In his handwriting—his lines and dashes, smudges and contours, that is to say—there is neither charm nor temperament. His colours do their work, saying what they have to say, but are without beauty in themselves or in their relations. There is something slightly depressing in the unlovely sincerity of his execution that reminds me rather of Fra Bartolomeo, and his imaginative limitations might be compared with those of Lesueur. I am taking a high standard, you perceive. And any one who cannot respond to the conviction and conscience with which he not only excludes whatever is irrelevant or fortuitous or false, but does positively realize his conceptions is, in my judgment, incapable of appreciating visual art.

No art could be more different from the art of Gertler than that of Duncan Grant. For him it seems impossible to scrabble a line or wipe his brush on a bit of paper without giving delight. As the saying goes, he is all over an artist. Men endowed with this prodigious sensibility, facility, and sense of beauty are not uncommon in England. In my time there have been four—Conder, Steer, John, and Duncan Grant. The danger is, of course, that they will fall into a trick of flicking off bits of empty prettiness to the huge contentment of a public that cannot bear artists to develop or be serious. But Duncan Grant shows no bad symptoms: from his early picture *Lemon Gatherers* (No. 35) (justly and almost universally admired for its great beauty and delightful references to Piero della Francesca) to the little "still life" in the north corner of the room, there is a vast progression; and beneath these gay and delicious paintings—so delicious one could fancy them good to eat—is a struggle with the problems of design and space-composition as vital as anything here to be found, unless it be in the work of Marchand. I noticed, by the way, that in *Lemon Gatherers*, a picture on cardboard, something is going wrong with the colours, and of this I take rather a serious view as the picture belongs to me. Duncan Grant is the hope of patriotic amateurs: blessed with adorable gifts and a powerful intellect, he should, if he has the strength to realize his conceptions and the courage to disdain popularity, become what we have been awaiting so long, an English painter in the front rank of European art.

Of the remaining British artists, the most interesting, to my mind, is Vanessa Bell. The influence of Duncan Grant on her work is unmistakable, and I hope, unlike most artists, who seem to suppose that for them the laws of cause and effect and the influence of environment are inoperative, she will not mind my saying so. Why, in artists so original as Giotto, El Greco, and Cézanne, at least 50 per cent is derivative! Vanessa Bell, like all artists, and especially women artists, is impressionable, but as the effect on her work of familiarity with one or two English painters and the modern French masters is altogether for the good, I see no harm in that. At the same time, she has very personal gifts. Besides a large simplicity of style, there is about her drawing something oddly sympathetic, and what I should call, for want of a better word, amusing; while a sense of the peculiar significance to her of certain forms and relations of forms comes through and gives to her work an air of intimacy that you will get from nothing else in this exhibition. Any woman who can make her work count in the art of her age deserves to be criticized very seriously. In literature the authoress stands firm on her own feet; only quite uneducated people—subaltern-poets and young Latin philosophers—believe that women cannot write; but it is a mere truism to say that no woman-painter, *pace* Madame Vigée-Lebrun, has yet held her own with contemporaries even. To-day there are at least three—Marie Laurencin, Goncharova, and Vanessa Bell—whose claim to take rank amongst the best of their generation will have to be answered very carefully by those who wish to disallow it. Behind them press half a dozen less formidable but still serious candidates, and I wish Mr. Fry would bring together a small collection of their works. It would be interesting to see how and how much they differ from the men; and, unless I mistake, it would effectively give the lie to those who fancifully conclude that because the Muses were women it is for women to inspire rather than create.

FOOTNOTE:

[20] This article was written for the *Nation*, but owing to a series of misfortunes could not be published until the exhibition was over. It then seemed best to reserve it for this collection.

CONTEMPORARY ART IN ENGLAND

Burlington Magazine July 1917

Only last summer, after going round the London galleries, a foreign writer on art whose name is as well known in America as on the Continent, remarked gloomily, and in private of course, that he quite understood why British art was almost unknown outside Great Britain. The early work of Englishmen, he admitted, showed talent and charming sensibility often, but, somehow or other, said he, their gifts fail to mature. They will not become artists, they prefer to remain British painters. They are hopelessly provincial, he said; and so they are.

Of our elder living artists—those, that is to say, who had found themselves and developed a style before the influence of Cézanne became paramount on the Continent—Mr. Sickert is probably the only one whom a continental amateur would dream of collecting; and he, be it noted, escaped early from British provincialism and plunged into the main stream of European art. On the other hand, the names of Mr. Steer, Mr. John, Mr. Orpen and Mr. McEvoy, here only less familiar than those of Cabinet Ministers or County Cricketers, abroad are as obscure. Mr. Steer, to be sure, has his portrait in the Uffizi, but then, as likely as not, the Poet Laureate has his birthday ode in the *Bibliothèque Nationale*. If Mr. Steer and Sir Edward Poynter are treated civilly abroad, that may be because England is an important country rather than because they are important artists.

No wonder patriots are vexed to find English art esteemed on the Continent and in America below the art of Germany or Scandinavia, seeing that English artists seem to possess more native sensibility than either Germans or Scandinavians and, perhaps, as much as Russians. Yet it is a fact that their work, by reason of its inveterate suburbanity, so wholly lacks significance and seriousness that an impartial historian, who could not neglect the mediocre products of North and East Europe, would probably dismiss English painting in a couple of paragraphs. For it is not only poor; it is provincial: and provincial art, as the historian well knows, never really counts.

It would be pleasant to fancy that England was working out, in isolation, an interesting and independent art; but clearly she is doing no such thing. There is no live tradition, nothing but fashions as stale as last week's newspaper. All that is alive is a private schoolboy rivalry, an ambition to be cock of the walk or to ape the cock, to be *primus inter pares* or *amico di primus*.

There is no live English tradition; and as English painters refuse obstinately to accept the European, and as artists do not spring up unaccountably as groundsel and dandelions appear to do, this is a rather serious misfortune. Art does not happen, it grows—not necessarily in the right direction. The fact that the development of art traced through schools and movements squares pretty well with historical fact proves conclusively the existence of "influences" in art. No one will deny that Botticelli was an original and extremely personal artist or that he is the obvious successor of Lippo Lippi. El Greco is called by some the most lonely figure in the history of art—yet it needs no wizard to divine that Titian was his master or that he was reared in the Byzantine tradition. Artists, though they hate being told so, are, in fact, like other things, subject to the law of cause and effect. Young artists, especially, are influenced by their surroundings and by the past, particularly the immediate past, by the men from five to thirty years older than themselves.

Art lives on tradition, of which contemporary culture is nothing but the last development. But English artists, for the most part, ignore the real tradition, and what passes for development here is no more, as a rule, than a belated change of fashion. All that is vital in modern art is being influenced by the French masters—Cézanne, Gauguin, Van Gogh, Matisse, Rousseau, Picasso, Bonnard, Maillol, who, in their turn, were influenced by the Impressionists, and who all have been nourished by that great French tradition which, of late, has been so surprisingly affected by the influx of Oriental art. English painting, however, has been left high and dry; and our younger men either imitate their teachers, too often second-rate drawing masters, enjoying at best a dull acquaintance with the Italian fifteenth and English eighteenth centuries, or, in revolt, set up for themselves as independent, hedgerow geniuses, ignorant, half-trained, and swollen by their prodigious conceit to such monsters as vastly astonish all those who can remember them as children.

It is worth noting, perhaps, that when men of talent make great men of themselves, wrapping up in the cloak of genius and fronting the world mysteriously, and when this attitude is tolerated by the public, there is reason to suspect that art fares ill. Since every extension lecturer knows that Raphael was part of a civilization greater than himself it seems unnecessary to treat a fashionable portrait-painter as though he were as inexplicable as an earthquake and as remote as the Matterhorn. One of the things to be desired in England is more respect for art and less reverence for artists.

English literature has a great tradition—the tradition of the greatest literature in the world. I say that in ignorance, to be sure, of Chinese, but not unmindful of Athenian. It would be inexact to describe that tradition as part of the main continental tradition which, since the middle of the seventeenth century, has been predominantly French, coloured in the eighteenth century by English, in the early nineteenth by German, and in the twentieth by Russian literature. Yet the English tradition, rich and splendid as it is, has never allowed itself for long to lose touch with the European current. The curious have only to turn from the works of our young writers to those of Nietzsche, Dostoievsky, Tchekov, Mallarmé, Rimbaud, Laforgue, and Claudel to appreciate the sensitiveness of English literature, which has never fallen into that insularity on which our lean visual art seems to pride itself. At moments—in mid-Victorian days, for instance—English literature may have appeared provincial; it was never suburban.

The tendency of British visual art to sink into a feeble barbarism seems to have existed always and to have asserted itself whenever we lost touch with the centre. The earliest English art, early Saxon sculpture, is good; it is a respectable part of that great Byzantine tradition which from the middle of the eighth to the middle of the ninth century appears to have been as vital in the north of England and in Ireland as in any part of Western Europe. The Normans kept England close to the centre and left us a little superb architecture; but from the beginning of the thirteenth century English visual art—architecture, painting, and sculpture—begins to take on that absurd air of being out of it which has since become the unfailing characteristic of an exhibition of home-made arts and crafts. In the seventeenth century we again got into touch with the movement and the genius of Inigo Jones and Wren gave us some admirable architecture. In the eighteenth we produced two painters of note, Blake and Crome, both of whom suffered desperately from their deplorable surroundings. What was interesting in Constable and Turner was seized and made use of more quickly and far more intelligently by French than by native artists. Here they were treated as isolated geniuses; there they were absorbed into the tradition of painting.

A student of contemporary art who found himself in the company of painters and amateurs in any great central city abroad—Paris, Stockholm, Copenhagen, Moscow, Munich, Vienna, Geneva, Milan, or Barcelona— would be able to discuss, and doubtless would discuss, the contemporary movement. That movement, as every one outside England seems to know, radiates from France. He would discuss, therefore, the respective merits of Matisse, Picasso, Marquet, Marchand, Friesz, Derain, Bonnard, de Vlaminck, Maillol, Laprade, Segonzac, Delaunay, etc. etc.; and not only discuss and criticize their works, but the direction in which each was moving, the influence of one on another, and the influence of Cézanne, Gauguin, Van Gogh, or the *douanier* Rousseau on all. Such a company would know something about the development of the movement in other countries; it would have something to say about Kandinsky and the Munich painters, about Goncharova and Larionoff, about the Barcelona school, and even about the Italian futurists. In a word, it would be able to talk about contemporary European painting. Only in an English studio would such conversation be hard to come by: there one might learn that Mr. Smith was a greater genius than Miss Jones, that Mrs. Robinson would never finish her picture in time for the New English Exhibition, that Mr. John was the greatest painter in the world—though Mr. Innes had once run him hard—and that the greatest sculptor was some one whose name I cannot recall. Of contemporary French painting at most a perfunctory word; yet to ignore it is to put oneself beyond the pale of contemporary culture. And there, it seems, is just where we must look for English art; in European civilization it has no place. It is out of it; it is suburban.

Educated people, enjoying some knowledge of what has been happening abroad during the last fifty years, can scarcely conceive the ignorance and insularity of contemporary British painters. It was only the other day that one of the best of them, fired by Mr. Roger Fry's article in the *Burlington Magazine*, walked into the National Gallery and saw for the first time a Renoir. He was duly impressed; and hurried off, I am glad to say, to buy a book of reproductions. Another promising painter, who was in Paris just before the war, not only never saw a Cézanne, a Gauguin, a Matisse or a Picasso, but was equally neglectful of the Impressionist masters, never taking the trouble to visit the Luxembourg and inspect the Caillebotte bequest. Imagine a continental man of science who in 1880 had never taken the trouble to read "The Origin of Species" or investigate the theory of evolution!

The state of mind produced in most English painters by this outlandish ignorance is calamitous. Unconscious of what is going on abroad, dimly, at best, aware of what has been done in the past, and lacking effective, well-informed criticism from writers in the newspapers and from their fellow-artists, they work without standards, ideals or artistic seriousness, and soon fall into that ghastly complacency in which a man is content to satisfy the market with endless repetition of some popular success. Modesty is a virtue hardly attainable by the prize student from the Slade or the Academy who is persuaded that in a few years he will be the prize painter of the world, and is, in a few years, by press and public duly confirmed in his delusion. His first ambition will be to get a picture accepted by the Royal Academy or the New English Art Club, his next to wheedle the quidnuncs—i.e. the newspaper men—into giving him a place amongst the local worthies, his last to discover a formula that shall be the strong-box of his lucky hit. This accomplished, commissions and paragraphs begin to roll in with comfortable regularity, and he rests replete—a leading British artist. Is he ever plagued with nightmares, I wonder, in which he dreams that outside England no competent amateur could possibly take him seriously?

Some British artists, when they were young—and some of them must once have been so—are said to have studied in Paris. Does it ever occur to them that their proper rivals, the men whose rivalry is stimulating and not merely disquieting, are not to be found in London? And does it occur to them that, instead of hunting for tips in Bond Street and Burlington House they might go for lessons to the National Gallery and South Kensington? Whatever people may think of the art of Henri Matisse, his fame is beyond cavil. Just before the war commissions and entreaties were pouring in on him, not from France only, but from Russia, Germany, Scandinavia, and America. He had—he has, for that matter—what no English painter, with the possible exception of Constable, ever had—a European reputation. Yet in the spring of 1914, looking with a friend at a picture by Chardin, he is said to have remarked that if he could believe that one day he would paint as good a thing as that he would be extremely happy. If one of our famous portrait-painters would go for once to the National Gallery and stand, not before a great master, but before a Philippe de Champaigne or a Vivarini, I wonder what he would say.

It is hard to conjecture; for our portrait-painters live in a world which, though not insensitive to prettiness, and impressed by obvious manifestations of ability, cares nothing for art or good painting. In such a world an artist—who is, after all, little better than a human being—can hardly be expected to develop his critical faculty. If some of our gifted men were to take their talents to Paris, where is a press and public that knows how to be serious about art, they would, one fancies, begin to feel dissatisfied with their facile triumphs and appetizing confections. They would feel, too, that they were surrounded by people who could recognize and appreciate conviction and science even though these were presented in forms too recondite for the mob. They would find that in Paris a painter can have praise enough without stooping for the applause of Mayfair. It is significant that, whereas English painters once they have found a style that hits the public taste, are not much inclined to change it, in Paris such an artist as Picasso, who has taken the fancy of amateurs and dealers in at least three different manners, goes on from experiment to experiment, leaving the public to follow as best it can.

But this difference between the atmosphere of London and of Paris brings up a question that had best be stated at once. What are the causes of British provincialism? Though its existence is a fact that runs right through the history of British art, it would be rash to assume that the causes have always been the same. For instance, the geographical isolation of England may at one time have been a cause; that has been removed by railways and steamboats. It will be sensible to speak in this article only of present causes of present ills.

Some people will have it that the insignificance of English art is very simply to be explained by a complete absence of native talent; but the mere inspection of English children's and students' work suffices to dispose of this too convenient hypothesis. In no country, perhaps, except France, is there more of that raw material from which good art is made. More plausible is the theory that the vast and towering greatness of English literature overhangs and starves all other forms of expression. In such a land as this it seems natural that any sense of art or power of creation should drift towards literature, and almost inevitable that the painters themselves should be half poets at heart, hardly convinced of the intrinsic value of their own medium, tending ever to substitute literary for plastic significance. Every critic is on the watch for a literary symbol and the chance of an allegorical interpretation, every cultivated amateur is eager to spy out an adroitly placed anecdote or shaft of pictorial satire; only with great pains is any one induced to regard a picture as an independent creation of form. In so literary a society it seems paradoxical almost to believe in pure painting; and, in despair, we cry out that no country can be expected to excel, at one time, in two arts. We forget Athens and Tuscany; we also forget France. For more than two hundred years France has led the visual art of Europe; and if English painting were ever to become one-tenth part as good as French literature I, for my part, should be as pleased as surprised. Of music I say nothing; yet in that art too France was beginning, just before the war, to challenge, not very formidably perhaps, the pre-eminence of Germany and to stand as the fair rival of Russia.

What hampers English artists most is, unless I mistake, the atmosphere in which they work. In France—in Germany too, they say—there is a fairly large, authoritative, and intensely serious public composed of artists, critics, and competent amateurs. This public knows so well what it is about that no painter, be he never so grandly independent, can make himself impervious to its judgments. It is an unofficial areopagus which imposes its decisions, unintentionally but none the less effectively, on the rich floating *snobisme* of Paris and of continental Europe. Those who go to the *Salon* for their art or invest in Henners and Bougereaus are reckoned hopelessly bourgeois even by the cultivated pressmen. It is a fastidious public, intelligent, learned, and extremely severe: painting it regards as an end in itself, not as a branch of journalism or a superior amenity; and no artist can begin to abuse his talent or play tricks with the currency without getting from this formidable body the sort of frown that makes even a successful portrait-painter wince. Indeed, many popular continental likeness-catchers, some of whom enjoy the highest honours in this country, having come under its ban, are now ruled out of contemporary civilization.[21] In England, on the other hand, the artist's public consists of that fringe of the fashionable world which dabbles in culture and can afford to pay long prices; from it the press obsequiously takes the cue; and any honest burgher who may wish to interest himself in the fine arts goes, I presume, for instruction to the place from which instruction comes—I mean the ha'penny papers.

Patronage of the arts in England is an expensive pleasure. In France the prices of the most promising young men range from one hundred to one thousand francs, and many an amateur with a first-rate collection of modern work has never paid more than five hundred francs for a picture. The Englishman who would possess the works of native geniuses must be able to put down from £50 to £2000. Thus it comes about that a few of the richer people in the more or less cultivated class form in England the artist's public. To them he must look for criticism, sympathy, understanding, and orders; and most of them, unluckily, have no use either for art or for good painting. What they want is furniture and a background—pretty things for the boudoir, handsome ones for the hall, and something jolly for the smoking-room. They want, not art, but amenity; whether they get it is another matter. What is certain is that their enthusiasms and disappointments, likes and dislikes, fancies and prejudices, have nothing whatever to do with art.

Behind the patrons and their decorators there is, of course, that odd little world sometimes called Bohemia, about which very little need be said. Every master, be he academician, New Englisher, or comic illustrator, is followed by a tail of lads and lasses whose business it is to sing the great man's praises and keep up, in the face of disheartening indifference, the pathetic tradition of British immorality. They give tips to the critics sometimes, but no one else marks them.

Such being the public, not unnaturally the more serious and independent painters endeavour to set up small coteries of their own as far from Mayfair and the Chelsea embankment as possible. Thus arose the Camden Town group under Mr. Sickert, thus arose the Friday Club and the London group. And here we may pause in our miserable and comminatory progress to admit gladly that in such societies are to be found plenty of talent and of what is much rarer, sincerity. Here are men who take art seriously; here are men who have no prospective sitter, no rich patron, no terrible drawing-master in mind; here are men to whom painting is the most important thing in the world. Unfortunately, in their isolation they are apt, like the rest, to come on the parish. Theirs is no vulgar provincialism; but in its lack of receptivity, its too willing aloofness from foreign influences, its tendency to concentrate on a mediocre and rather middle-class ideal of honesty, it is, I suspect, typically British. There is nothing Tennysonian about these men, nothing Kiplingesque; their art is neither meretricious nor conceited; but it reminds one oddly of perpendicular architecture.

These are the men that might profit by good criticism, for they are intelligent and fair-minded. Alas! English criticism is more woefully out of it than painting even. The ignorance of our critics is appalling.[22] Seven years ago there was brought over to London a collection of pictures by Cézanne, Gauguin, and Van Gogh. Every man and woman on the Continent who claimed acquaintance with modern art had already come to some conclusion about these painters whose works were in the public collections of Germany and the North and in the private collections of directors of French galleries. Some thought that they took rank amongst the very great painters of the world; others that there was a general disposition to overrate them; no one denied that they were considerable men or that Cézanne was a master. In London no one had heard of them, so it was decided out of hand that they were immoral aliens fit only to be thrown on the nearest bonfire. Cézanne was a butcher, Gauguin a *farceur*, Van Gogh a particularly disagreeable lunatic: that is what the critics said, and the public said "Hee-haw." They reminded one of a pack of Victorian curates to whom the theory of natural selection had been too suddenly broken. Two years later Roger Fry and I collected and arranged at the Grafton Galleries an exhibition of contemporary French art—Matisse, Picasso, Maillol, etc. Every one abroad had recognized these men as interesting artists of varying merit; no one doubted that the movement they represented was significant and of promise. Only the English critics had learnt nothing. They never do; they only teach. Here was something going on under their noses that might well turn out to be as important as the early fifteenth-century movement in Tuscany, and they went on directing the attention of their pupils to the work of Alfred Stevens. Here was the art of the East—of China, Persia, and Turkestan—being revealed to us by European scholars, and they went on messing about with English choir-stalls and sanctuary-rings.

Our critics and teachers provided, and continue to provide, an artistic education comparable with the historical education provided by our board-schools. People who have been brought up to believe that the history of England is the history of Europe—that it is a tale of unbroken victory, leadership, and power—feel, when they hear of the ascendancy of France or of the House of Austria or of the comparative insignificance of England till the dawn of the eighteenth century, angry first and then incredulous. So they give themselves the least possible chance of hearing such unpalatable nonsense by living snugly in the slums and suburbs, where, persuaded that they have nothing to learn from damned foreigners, they continue to entertain each other with scraps of local and personal gossip. That is what our art criticism sounds like to cultivated people from abroad.

A few months ago an extraordinarily fine Renoir, a recognized masterpiece of modern art, was hung in the National Gallery. Any young painter who may have seen and profited by it need not thank those directors of public taste, the critics. It was passed by in silence or with a nod by the bulk of our paid experts, who were much more pleased by a particularly poor but very large Puvis, which possibly reminded them in some obscure way of a pre-Raphaelite picture.[23] But when there was question of selling a block of unimportant water-colours by our national Turner and buying with the proceeds two or three great masterpieces of Italian art the hubbub of these patriot-geese rose for a moment above the noise of battle. Such is the atmosphere in which young British artists are expected to mature.

One wonders what is going to happen to them—these young or youngish Englishmen of talent. There are at least half a dozen on whom a discerning critic would keep a hopeful eye—Mr. Duncan Grant, Mr. Lewis, Mr. Stanley Spenser, Mr. Gertler, Mr. Roberts, Mr. Bomberg, Mrs. Bell, and Mr. Epstein—for it would be absurd to omit from this list an artist possessed of such skill, scholarship, and surprising powers of improvisation and development as the last-named. Of these some already have been touched by that breath of life which, blowing from Paris, has revolutionized painting without much discomposing the placid shallows of British culture. Standing in the broad light of European art, these can hardly detect that sacred taper which the New English Art Club is said to shield from the reactionary puffings of the Royal Academy. And, although it is a dangerous thing in the suburbs to ignore nice points of precedence and venerable feuds, such magnanimity makes for progress. Mr. Grant, Mr. Lewis, Mr. Epstein, and Mrs. Bell, at any rate, are all cut by Tooting, for they have seen the sun rise and warmed themselves in its rays; it is particularly to be regretted, therefore, that Mr. Lewis should have lent his great powers to the canalizing (for the old metaphor was the better) of the new spirit in a little backwater called English vorticism, which already gives signs of becoming as insipid as any other puddle of provincialism. Can no one persuade him to be warned by the fate of Mr. Eric Gill, who, some ten years ago, under the influence presumably of Malliol, gave arresting expression to his very genuine feelings, until, ridden by those twin hags insularity and wilful ignorance, he drifted along the line of least resistance and, by an earnest study of English ecclesiastical ornament, reduced his art to something a little lower than English alabasters? The danger is there always; and unless our able young men make a grand struggle, they too will find themselves sucked into the backwater, impotent, insignificant, and prosperous.

It is not treasonable, I think, to hope that the war will some day be over. And let no one imagine that when the war is over it will be found that the new movement in France is dead or dying. In little periodicals, photographs, brochures, letters, and stray works that from time to time cross the Channel there is plenty of evidence that it is as vital as ever. Even a European war cannot kill a thing of that sort. The question is whether, after the war, young English artists will realize that they too, by reason of their vocation, of the truth that is in them, belong to a communion wider and far more significant than the conventicle to which they were bred. England, we hear, is to wake up after the war and take her place in a league of nations. May we hope that young English artists will venture to take theirs in an international league of youth? That league existed before the war; but English painters appear to have preferred being pigmies amongst cranes to being artists amongst artists. *Aurons-nous changé tout ça? Qui vivra verra.* The league exists; its permanent headquarters are in Paris; and from London to Paris is two hundred and fifty miles—a journey of seven and a half hours in times of peace.

FOOTNOTES:

[21] Since these words were written the British Press, or the Government maybe, has had the bright idea of interning one of them. To be sure he was a very bad painter; but the punishment seems rather severe for an offence which usually incurs nothing worse than a knighthood.

[22] There are, of course, exceptions. The critics of the *Times*, the *Westminster Gazette*, and the *Evening Standard*, for instance, are neither ignorant nor stupid; but they are all, one fancies, hampered by nervous and ill-educated editors.

[23] I have referred already to Mr. Roger Fry's article in the *Burlington Magazine*, and would draw attention also to his article in the *Nation*.

ART AND WAR[24]

An acquaintance of mine, a French artist, who used to live in England and paint pictures for which I care nothing but on which the cultured dote, started early in August to join his regiment, leaving behind him his wife and five children. So miserable was the prospect before these that a benevolent lady wrote to such of her rich friends as happened to be amateurs of painting praying them to buy a picture or two and so help the family of their unfortunate favourite. One and all refused, severely giving the lady to understand that this was no time to think about art. Of charity they said nothing; but they were generous, I dare say, in some more patriotic and conspicuous fashion.

Charity, however, is beside my point. What interests me in this little story is the unanimity with which the cultivated people agree that this is no time for art. It interests me because I have lately been taken to task for saying that the cultured regard art as no more than an elegant amenity. The war has put my opinion to the proof and I am shocked to discover how much I was in the right. From every quarter comes the same cry—"This is no time for art!" Those galleries and exhibitions which are not closed are visited chiefly by homeless refugees; if literary taste goes beyond the newspapers it is only to salute the verse of Mr. Begbie and the prose of Mr. H. G. Wells; even at concerts our ears are exasperated by national platitudes and the banalities of our Allies. This is no time for art. Good taste is unpatriotic; the man who continues to care for painting, poetry, or music is little better than a Hun.

That people who in times of peace treat art as an amenity should feel that this is no time for art is, I suppose, natural. That they should expect those who feel that art is the most important thing in the world to do the same seems to me unreasonable. To those who care seriously for art, to those for whom it is a constant source of passionate emotion, the notion that this is no time for art seems as ludicrous as to a Christian mystic of the ninth century would have seemed the notion that that tortured age was no time for religious ecstasy. People who are capable of ecstasy, be it religious or æsthetic, are apt to distinguish between ends and means. They know that empires and dominations, political systems and material prosperity and life itself are valuable only as means to those states of mind which alone are good as ends. Thus it comes about that the things which to the majority are of primary importance, because to the majority they seem to be ends, are to a handful of mystics and artists of secondary importance because to them they are no more than means. They cannot forget about art and think exclusively about war, because if they forgot about art the world and its ways would seem unworthy of thought. Public activities and operations they feel are of consequence only in so far as they affect the things that matter—the raptures of art and religion, that is to say, and abstract thought and personal relations.

It is not reasonable to expect us to turn our backs on absolute good and consider exclusively what may be a means to good. Besides, we could not do so if we would. The artist must think more about art, the philosopher more about truth, the mystic more about God, the æsthete more about beauty, and the lover, they tell me, more about the beloved, than about anything else. The fact is, we are not practical people; we cannot adjust ourselves to circumstances, so we must be content to appear imprudent and unpatriotic. We are not masters of our fate; not only have we got hold of what we believe to be the greatest thing in the world, the greatest thing in the world has got hold of us.

A crisis has divided the sheep from the goats—I care not on which hand I am marshalled—and now we know who are the people that love art because they must and who love it because they think they ought to. I am making no moral judgment; I am pointing out merely that those who say "This is no time to think about art" admit that for them thinking or not thinking about art is a matter of choice. I have always supposed that it was perfectly well with one who had lost himself in an ecstasy of creation or contemplation. How can he be better off who has already attained beatitude? To invite such a one to relinquish the best and bestir himself about what may be a means to good seems to me absurd. That has always been my opinion and I cannot conceive the circumstances that would compel me to change it. Those who reject it, those who deny that certain states of mind, amongst which is the state of æsthetic contemplation, are alone good as ends, will find themselves in an intellectual position which appears to me untenable: I shall not quarrel with them, however, so long as they leave us alone and refrain from cant. According to them there are better things than Beauty or Truth or the contemplation of either. I simply disagree: it is only when I catch them wringing their hands over the ruins of Reims that I protest.

Take not the name of art in vain: at least be ashamed to use it for political purposes. Any stick may be good enough to beat Germans with. Beat them if you can: I shall have no tears for them and their strong military government. It is not people like me who will weep for Prussia. But, though any stick may be good enough, some are too good. Besides, however much we love France and the French, let us have the justice to remember that if, as seems possible, French soldiers were using the cathedral as a post of observation, the Germans, according to what are called the rules of war, were in the right. In that case it was the French themselves who first transgressed that law which, they now tell us, makes neutral and inviolate works of art. For my own part, I utterly deny that it can ever, in any circumstances, be right to destroy or put in jeopardy beautiful things. But for any of those governments which took a hand in the deliberate ruin of the summer palace at Pekin to prate of vandalism and pose as defenders of art is not only disingenuous but silly. The spectacle of European soldiers and statesmen who, to admonish such evil Chinamen as might persist in defending their liberty and their religion, destroyed without demur the masterpieces of Oriental art, the spectacle, I say, of these people whimpering over the late Gothic of Louvain or the early Gothic of Reims, strikes me as being what the French, if their sense of humour had not suffered more than their monuments, would call *un peu trop fort*.

Reims is, or was—I am not sure whether we are more conscious of what existed before the bombardment or of what we imagine remains—Reims is or was a typical thirteenth-century building; and, like most thirteenth-century buildings, is or was, to my feeling, of no great artistic significance. That it is a venerable focus of sentiment no one denies; so, I suppose, is the monstrosity of Cologne and the Albert Memorial. I am not concerned with sentiment, but with art. Therefore, I must note that of such artistic value as the cathedral ever possessed the greater part was not destroyed by the German bombardment: it was destroyed when, some years ago, the upper part of the church was made as good as new by the Ministry of Fine Arts. Only the glass, and the sculpture over the little door in the north transept, and a few twelfth-or very early thirteenth-century figures which had escaped restoration will be a great loss to the world; and, for our comfort, we may remember that the glass was not comparable with the glass at Chartres or Bourges, while finer sculpture is to be seen in scores of Romanesque churches. I can listen with admirable patience to tales of damage done to Reims cathedral; but should the abbey church of St. Remi have been injured it would be less easy to pardon the responsible party. St. Remi is a masterpiece of the eleventh century, and was still, when last I saw it, a work of splendour and significance in spite of having suffered at the hands of French architects worse things than it is likely to have suffered from German gunners.

It is a mistake for the English upper classes to assure the world that they prize a work of art above a victory; the world knows better. Are not these the people who were telling us just now that this was no time for art? Is it seemly in them, is it prudent even, to revile their own class in Germany for caring as little about art as themselves? When the Germans sacked Louvain and shelled Reims our politicians and press discovered suddenly that art is a sacred thing and that people who disrespect it are brutes. Agreed: and how have the moneyed classes in England respected art? What sacrifices, material, moral or military, have they made? Here, in the richest country in the world, with what difficulty do we raise a few thousand pounds to buy a masterpiece. What institution do we starve so abjectly as we starve the National Gallery? Has any one met a rich man who denied himself a motorcar to keep a genius? How dare the people who fill our streets and public places with monuments that make us the laughing-stock of Europe, the people who cannot spare a few guineas to save a picture, who cheerfully improve away respectable architecture, who allow artists to perish and put up the Admiralty Arch—how dare such people pose as the champions of culture and expose their wounded feelings in the penny and halfpenny papers. In times of peace they used art as a hobby and a means of self-advertisement, in wartime they would brandish it as a stick against their foes. The old abuse was vulgar, the new one is worse.

We can measure the sensibility of these politic amateurs when we overhear their chatter about patriotic art and catch them, as we caught them lately, attempting to ban German music. "Give us patriotic art," they cry. As if art could be patriotic or unpatriotic! One might as well cry for patriotic mathematics. The essence of art is that it provokes a peculiar emotion, called æsthetic, which, like religious emotion or the passion for truth, transcends nationality. Art's supreme importance lies precisely in this: its glory is to share with truth and religion the power of appealing to that part of us which is unconditioned by time or place or public or personal interests. A work of art satisfies us æsthetically, just as a true proposition satisfies us intellectually, whether it was made in Germany or elsewhere: by whom it was created, when it was created, and where it was created are matters of no consequence to any one but an archæologist.

There is no such thing as patriotic art. The qualities in a poem, a picture, or a symphony that lead people to describe the work as patriotic are purely adventitious and have nothing to do with its æsthetic significance. Wordsworth's so-called patriotic sonnets, in so far as they are works of art—and what superb works of art they are!—are as appreciable in Berlin as in London. They appeal as directly to the æsthetic sensibility of any German who can read English and appreciate poetry as to the sensibility of an Englishman; and unless a man be æsthetically sensitive he will never really appreciate them no matter where he was born. The state of mind which art provokes and which comprehends and reacts to art is one in which nationality has ceased to exist. I am not saying that an ardent patriot cannot appreciate art; I say that when he appreciates it he is carried into a world in which patriotism becomes meaningless. If he has not been carried into that world he has not appreciated art. I shall not deny that at the present moment an Englishman may find something peculiarly sympathetic in the ideas and memories associated with the poetry of Wordsworth. It is conceivable that a Frenchman may find unpalatable certain memories and ideas associated with the music, or more probably with the name, of Bach. But these memories and ideas are not a part of the music; they are only the contribution of an unæsthetic auditor. The man who says that he can no longer appreciate the music of Bach merely admits that he has never appreciated the music of any one.

Two things above all others give value to a civilization, art and thought. It were well that those even who cannot appreciate Beauty and Truth should bear this in mind. Instead of blustering about this being no time for art they should rejoice that there are some who, rising above tumultuous circumstance, continue to create and speculate. So long as a sense of art and the disinterested passion for truth persist, the world retains some right to respectful consideration; once these disappear its fate becomes a matter of indifference. The continued existence of a stupid and insensitive world, incapable of æsthetic rapture or metaphysical ecstasy, is not particularly desirable. It may be wise to wage war for the sake of civilization; that is a question of probabilities with which I am not at present concerned: but a war that leaves the world poorer in art or thought is, whatever its political consequences, a victory for barbarism and for humanity a disaster. A nation that would defend the cause of civilization must remain civilized; and that a nation may emerge civilized from fierce and exhausting war, that it may preserve unabated its power for good, it is necessary that during its horrid and circumscribing labours there should have been men who, detached and undismayed, continued to serve interests higher and wider than the interests of any State or confederacy. In times of storm and darkness it is the part of artists and philosophers to tend the lamp. This duty they perform unconsciously by simply minding their own business.

Artists and philosophers and those who are apt to handle truth and beauty are, in fact, the vestals of civility. To be sure, they are not appointed or elected, neither are they consecrate nor shorn nor always chaste; nevertheless, they tend the lamp. Because they alone can project their thoughts and feelings far beyond the frontiers of States and Empires, because their sympathies and interests are universal, because they can lose themselves in timeless abstractions, because their kingdom is not of this world, they alone in times of division and calamity and shortsighted passion can keep the flame alive. Thus do they unintentionally serve the State. So far as they are concerned their beneficence is quite adventitious, their service supererogatory. For they do not live to serve humanity, but to serve their masterful and inhuman passion; by serving that faithfully they save the world. Let them continue to think and feel, watching, untroubled, the cloudless heavens, till men, looking up from their beastly labours, again catch sight of the unchanging stars.

Mens equa in arduis: calm and unconcerned in the hurricane: the mind set steadily on indestructible things: that, I think, is how it should be in these days with artists and philosophers. When the Roman soldiers entered Syracuse they found Archimedes absorbed in a mathematical problem. He never raised his head and they killed him where he sat.

I want to save those nice, cultivated people who go about saying that this is no time for art from doing some harm and making themselves ridiculous. To them, not to the artists, is my mission. They are in danger of becoming coarse and absurd and of saying things that their enemies will never allow them to forget. They are not formidable: besides, art is fearless. For art cannot die; neither can the desire for art. If history teaches nothing else worth remembering, it teaches that. Artists will create though they must starve for it, and art we will have though our days be numbered. Artists and those who care for art may be a mere handful in the human mass, but theirs is the passionate faith that conquers somehow in spite of battles and holds the world in fee.

Art survives: the state of this chilly, quarrelsome little planet has never grown so desperate that artists have lost faith. After all, why should they? Art is not less important because some men are bad and most are wretched; and it is no part of an artist's business to straighten out the contortions of humanity. "The loss of hue to river-banks," observed Ch'êng Hao, the Sung poet, "is the river-banks' affair." Art has seen worse days than these. Between 937 and 1059, if we may believe Glaber, there were forty-eight years of pestilence and famine. From Constantinople to Exeter the world was one miserable sore. Cannibalism became chronic. In the market-place of Tournus human joints were exposed for sale. Man had sunk to such depths of impotence that the wolves came out and disputed with him the mastery of Europe. War seems to have been the only activity for which the leaders of the people were not too feeble: let us hope that they kept honour bright and preserved nicely the balance of Neustria, Austria, and the kingdom of Italy. And over all hung, as well it might, the terror of judgment and the end of the world. Yet art survived. The years that lie round about the millennium are precisely those in which artists seem to have been unable almost to do wrong. Then it was that the æsthetic sense, rising calm above confusion, detached and remote from human woes, expressed itself gravely in that early Romanesque architecture and sculpture which remains the imperishable glory of the Middle Age.

There have been wars as great as this; there may be greater. Empires and continents have gone down and may again go down into misery. Art survives. What remains of Egypt but her monuments? In Babylonia there were kings and princes before the coming of the Assyrians; there were statesmen, generals, and priests: but the glory and story of that land would be for us a vague, bad dream were it not that the sculpture of the vanquished Sumerians remains splendid and unobscure. Kublai Khan, that conquerer of China and scourge of all the East, lives, if he live at all, in the verse of an English poet, while the art of the people he came to destroy is the great glory of Asia and the inspiration of half the world.

To be or not to be thinking about art is not a matter of choice. Art is imperious. As well tell an artist not to breathe as not to create. Artists will be artists; and so far as I can see the spirit has never foundered in the wreck of material things. If those ancient ministers of the devil, fire and sword, pestilence and famine, could not force men to stop creating and feeling, I do not suppose that journalists and politicians and inactive colonels and fire-eating curates will be more successful. There never was a time that was no time for art. In the darkness of the darkest ages the æsthetic sense shines clear. Were not the masterpieces of Attic comedy written in a beleagured State in the throes of a disastrous war? And was it not in 1667 that England suffered what has been called her greatest humiliation? Certainly it was in 1667 she received her greatest epic.

Few, indeed, can look steadily at their own times. To the ephemera that tossed on the waters of the past the ripples were mountainous; to us the past is a sad, grey lake, scarcely ruffled, from which emerge the tall lights of art and thought. It must be a defective sense of proportion, I think, that makes people who cite Aristophanes, but never heard of Conon, who are deep in *Paradise Lost* but neither know nor care who won the battle of Lowestoft, assert so confidently that this is no time for art. Let them, for their own sakes, consider what sort of figure in history one would cut who had adjured young Shakespeare—thirty years of age and, if one may draw inferences from tradition, able at least to shoot—to give over his precious fooling and join the expeditionary force in Portugal. Yet the moment was grave: we had lost *The Revenge* and failed ignominiously before Cadiz; we still expected invasion. Shakespeare and the rest of them might surely have done something for their country.

FOOTNOTE:

[24] This essay was written for a Hampstead literary society—I forget the name—and read some time in October 1914. It was printed the following year in the *International Journal of Ethics*.

BEFORE THE WAR

Cambridge Magazine May 1917

It is to me a strange thing that since the beginning of the war Utopia-building has gone on more merrily than ever. Almost every one has a scheme for social reconstruction; and of these schemes, though most are of that familiar kind which discovers in compulsory strike-arbitration the true and only panacea, some are in themselves attractive enough, being more or less intelligent attempts to combine Socialist economics with the maximum of personal liberty. And yet I can take no interest in any of them, though my apathy, I know, vexes my friends who complain that in old days, before the war, no castle-builder was more reckless than I.

Very true: but things have changed since then. Before the war England was immensely rich; and the upper classes, before the war, were beginning to find barbarism boring. Consequently the lower and lower-middle, as they got money and pushed up towards the light, entered a world that could afford to be liberal, about which floated, vaguely enough, ideas that in time might have been turned to good account. That is where the Edwardian-Georgian age differed most hopefully from the Victorian. In Victorian days when a man became rich or ceased to be miserably poor he still found himself in a society where money-making was considered the proper end of existence: intellectually he was still in the slums. In the spring of 1914 society offered the new-comer precisely what the new-comer wanted, not cut-and-dried ideas, still less a perfect civilization, but an intellectual flutter, faint and feverish no doubt, a certain receptivity to new ways of thinking and feeling, a mind at least ajar, and the luxurious tolerance of inherited wealth. Not, I suppose, since 1789 have days seemed more full of promise than those spring days of 1914. They seem fabulous now, and a fairy-tale never comes amiss.

The generation that takes its first look at the world in the years that follow the war will hardly be persuaded that in the years that just preceded it the governing class was drifting out of barbarism. Yet so it was. The brighter and better educated, at any rate, were beginning to discover that clever people are more entertaining than stupid ones, and that social experiment is as good an extravagance as another. England was fantastically rich; and some of the very rich allowed some of the very clever to wheedle from them great sums of money, knowing all the time that these would be applied to such unsettling activities as the education of thankless labourers or anti-sweating propaganda. Even towards Art rolled a few coppers; indeed, the best painter in England tells me that about this time he was earning as much as two hundred a year. It was thought odd but not shameful in Mr. Thomas Beecham to spend some part of his father's fortune on producing modern music and the operas of Mozart. In fact, it was coming to be a question whether there was anything essentially ridiculous about a musician, a poet, or a Socialist. *Punch* was rarely seen in the best houses. For a few dizzy years it was wildly surmised that to found a civilization might be as thrilling as to found a family, and that one could be as romantic and snobbish about Art as about bull-dogs or battleships. To be open-minded became modish; people with interesting, subversive things to say were encouraged to talk—always provided they talked with an air of not taking quite seriously what they said. The poor were repressed as firmly as ever, but the job was left to such paid bullies as constables, magistrates, and judges, whom the nicer patricians employed, but took leave to despise.

In 1914 what in England is called "Society" gave promise of becoming what it had not been since the French Revolution—something that a fastidious person could tolerate. It was becoming open-minded. Now open-mindedness is the *sine qua non* of what is called "brilliant society," and brilliant society is by far the best manure with which to fertilize the soil in which revolutions are to be cultivated. Only when Society becomes clever and inquisitive, and wants to be amused, does it open its doors to reformers, and only in such society can most reformers—reformers, that is to say, who have not been born with an exceptional gift of self-criticism—acquire that sense of humour and dash of cynicism lacking which they perish.

Society to be good must be open-minded; without that there can be neither wit nor gaiety nor conversation worth the name. Prejudices and pruderies, respect of persons, reverence of sentiments, and consideration for the corns of the dull are fatal. On such terms even fun and high spirits soon degenerate to buffoonery and romps. There must be no closed subjects at the mention of which faces lengthen, voices become grave, and the air thickens with hearty platitudes: the intellect must be suffered to play freely about everything and everybody. Wit is the very salt and essence of society, and you can no more have wit that hurts nothing Queen Victoria respected than you can have truth that hurts nothing she believed. Now wit is purely an affair of the intellect, and so is society when it is at all good; no one but a fool dreams of going there for fine feelings and profound emotions. But the intellect to be nimble must be free: 'tis a sprite will play you the prettiest tricks an you give it the run of the house; close but one door though, and it sits sulking in the lobby. Delightful are the games it can play you: wit, irony, criticism, thrilling ideas, visions of fantastic anarchy and breathless generalizations—all these it can give; but the earth and all things above and below must be its toy-box; from the deferential intellect expect nothing better than puns, anecdotes, comfortable platitudes, elaborate facetiousness, and the *Saturday Westminster.*

I do not suggest that in the spring of 1914 English society was brilliant or anything of that sort: I think it was tired of being merely decent. One or two fine ladies had made open-mindedness and a taste for ideas fashionable: *snobisme* was doing the rest. And we may as well recognize, without more ado, that, Athens and Florence being things of the past, a thick-spread intellectual and artistic *snobisme* is the only possible basis for a modern civilization. Thanks chiefly to the emergence of a layer of this rich and rotten material one had hopes in 1914 of some day cultivating a garden in which artists and writers would flourish and prophets learn not to be silly. Society before the war showed signs of becoming what French society before the Revolution had been—curious, gay, tolerant, reckless, and reasonably cynical. After the war I suppose it will be none of these things. Like the eighteenth century, having learnt its lesson, it will borrow a sober tone and simpler tastes from the *bourgeoisie.*

For the Edwardian culture did not go very deep; the country gentlefolk and elder business men, the middling professionals and half-pay officers, never abandoned the Victorian tradition. They could not but deplore the imprudence of their too affable leaders, whom, nevertheless, it was their duty and pleasure to admire. They knew that Mr. Balfour was addicted to the plays of Bernard Shaw, that Anatole France had been entertained at the Savoy, and that Cunninghame Graham—a man who was once sent to prison for rioting—sat down to dinner at the tables of the nobility. It made them uneasy and irritable; it also made them fancy that they, too, should keep abreast of the times. So they let their wives subscribe to some advanced fashion-paper with Beardsleyesque-Brunelleschi drawings and felt, quite rightly, that it was rather nasty. The heart of England was sound. All over the country were homes in which ladies were permitted neither to smoke cigarettes nor read the plays of Ibsen nor pronounce, without a shudder, the name of Mr. Lloyd George. By the majority the use of cosmetics was still reckoned a sin, Wagner a good joke, and Kipling a good poet. The *Spectator* was still read. Nevertheless, the student of paulo-pre-war England will have to recognize that for a few delirious years a part of the ruling faction—cosmopolitan plutocrats and some of the brisker peeresses—listened more willingly to the clever than to the good. There was a veneer of culture or, as I have hinted, of intellectual *snobisme.*

Heaven may delude those whom it wills to destroy, but the very infirmities of its favourites it shapes to their proper advantage. The governing classes of Europe effectually upset the apple-carts of their fanciful friends by getting into a war. When that happened these dream-pedlars surely should have perceived that the game was up. They had always known that only by devoting its first half to the accumulation of wealth and culture could the twentieth century hope in its second to make good some part of its utopic vision. Wealth was the first and absolute necessity: Socialism without money is a nightmare. To live well man must be able to buy some leisure, finery, and elbow-room. Anything is better than a poverty-stricken communism in which no one can afford to be lazy or unpractical.

If, as seems probable, the energies of Europe during the next fifty years must be devoted to re-amassing the capital that Europe has squandered, the concentration on business will be as fatal to the hopes of social reformers as the poverty that provokes it. One foresees the hard, unimaginative view of life regaining the ascendancy, laborious insensibility re-crowned queen of the virtues, "Self-help" by Smiles again given as a prize for good conduct, and the grand biological discovery that the fittest to survive do survive adduced again as an argument against income-tax. When one remembers the long commercial tyranny that followed the Napoleonic wars, the tyranny under which money-making became the chief duty of man, under which Art foundered and middle-class morality flourished, one grows uneasy. And if one cannot forget the stragglers from the Age of Reason, the old, pre-Revolutionary people who, in the reign of Louis XVIII, cackled obsolete liberalism, blasphemed, and span wrinkled intrigues beneath the scandalized brows of neo-Catholic grandchildren, one becomes exceedingly sorry for oneself.

Even before the war we were not such fools as to suppose that a new world would grow up in a night. First had to grow up a generation of civilized men and women to desire and devise it. That was where the intellectual dilettanti came in. Those pert and unpopular people who floated about propounding unpleasant riddles and tweaking up the law wherever it had been most solemnly laid down were, in fact, making possible the New Age. Not only did they set chattering the rich and gibbering with rage the less presentable revolutionaries, it was they who poured out the ideas that filtered through to the trades-union class; and, if that class was soon to create and direct a brand-new State, it was high time that it should begin to handle the sort of ideas these people had to offer. Doubtless the trade-unionists would have developed a civilization sweeter and far more solid than that which flitted so airily from *salon* to studio, from Bloomsbury to Chelsea; before long, I dare say, they would have dismissed our theories as heartless and dry and absurd to boot; in the end, perhaps, they would have had our heads off—but not, I think, until they had got some ideas into their own. The war has ruined our little patch of civility as thoroughly as a revolution could have done; but, so far as I can see, the war offers nothing in exchange. That is why I take no further interest in schemes for social reconstruction.

THE END

PRESS OPINIONS ON
"ART" BY CLIVE BELL

"A book of absorbing interest. No one who reads it will, I am sure, find the brief and somewhat comprehensive title either arrogant or misleading. It contains some of the profoundest, truest and most courageous considerations stated with connected and well-supported conviction. The book is not only racy and readable, but—rarest of all things on this subject—it is comprehensible. The value of the book as an illuminant to thought on painting is henceforth impossible to ignore."—Mr. WALTER SICKERT in the *New Age*.

"Certainly one of the most brilliant, provocating, suggestive things that have ever been written on the subject. What a breath of fresh air this iconoclast brings in with him, what masses of mouldy snobbism he sweeps into the dust-heap, how salutary even for the idols themselves is such a thorough turning out! It will be seen that this is a book that all who care for art must read; the surprising good fortune that has befallen them is that it is so eminently readable."—Mr. ROGER FRY in the *Nation*.

"By reason of its originality of thought and virility of expression Mr. Clive Bell's "Art" is entitled to rank as a remarkable contribution to the literature of art. The contemporary movement has found no abler defender and exponent."—*Glasgow Herald*.

"Lovers of art owe Mr. Clive Bell thanks for the most stimulating, not to say the most provoking, book on art that has recently appeared."—*Athenæum*.

"Mr. Bell says many wise and witty things. Few people will agree with them all, many will get angry with the remorselessness of his logic, but nobody can read the book through carefully without clearing up their own minds on the subject and incidentally acquiring a sounder understanding of what art is and means."—*Sunday Times*.

"He utters paradoxes as if they were the tritest things in the world; all epigram and impudence he trails his coat assiduously, and, while his brilliance is vastly entertaining, his method of bouncing us into liking what he likes, and hating what he hates, is likely to infuriate quite as many readers as it takes by storm."—*Manchester Guardian*.

"The rather sterile literature of art criticism has been seriously enriched by a brilliant if wilful manifesto. The refreshing absence of obscurity common to art criticism will be particularly welcome. For genuine students the book possesses significant form, and will be indispensable."— *Westminster Gazette.*

"This is the best and most entertaining book about art that we have ever read."—*Standard.*

"This book is of first-rate importance. But nobody need be frightened of it on that account. Unlike most important works on the theory of art, it is thoroughly entertaining from beginning to end. Its main thesis is a generalization which, if true, is applicable to all schools and all epochs. The book is stimulating and suggestive."—*Cambridge Review.*

"Mr. Bell's book has been generally recognized as the most interesting and stimulating appreciation that has yet appeared in this country of the movement which we call post-impressionism. The book is, however, much wider in its scope. A book upon æsthetics at once serious (on the whole), sane, and extremely entertaining."—*Welsh Outlook.*

Milton Keynes UK
Ingram Content Group UK Ltd.
UKHW021559260524
443160UK00005B/370